Kiera Clayton Travel Guide To

Hurghada
EGYPT

KIERA CLAYTON

COPYRIGHT NOTICE

No part of this publication may be reproduced, distributed, or transmitted in any form or by any means, including photocopying, recording, or other electronic or mechanical methods, without the prior written permission of the Author, except in the case of brief quotations embodied in critical reviews and certain other non-commercial uses permitted by copyright law.

DISCLAIMER

The information provided in this publication is intended for educational purposes only. It has been sourced from materials believed to be reliable at the time of publication. However, the opinions and information contained herein are subject to change without prior notice.

Readers acknowledge that the Author/Publisher is not offering legal, financial, or professional advice. The Publisher/Author makes no guarantees as to the accuracy, completeness, or adequacy of the information provided.

The Publisher assumes no responsibility for any errors, omissions, or misinterpretations of the information presented. The Publisher/Author expressly disclaims liability for any consequences arising from the use or application of the material contained in this book.

TABLE OF CONTENT

Copyright Notice ii
Disclaimer iii
Table of Content iv
Introduction 12
Introduction to Hurghada 12
    Overview of Hurghada 12
    History and Culture of Hurghada 13
    Why Visit Hurghada? 14
    What Makes Hurghada Unique? 15

Chapter 1 17
How to Get There 17
    Nearest Airports 17
    Transport Options from the Airport 18
    Traveling by Car: Rentals and Driving Tips 19
    Public Transportation Options 20

Chapter 2 22
Best Time to Visit and Duration of Stay 22
    Hurghada's Climate 22
    Best Seasons to Visit 23
    Ideal Duration of Stay for Different Types of Travelers 24
    Special Events and Festivals 25

Chapter 3 28
Transportation Within Hurghada 28
    Getting Around by Public Transport 28
    Renting Bicycles and Electric Scooters 29
    Local Buses and Shared Taxis 31
    Car Rentals and Driving in the City 32

Chapter 4 34
Top 10 Tourist Attractions 34
    Giftun Islands 34
    Hurghada Marina 35
    El Gouna 35
    Desert Safari Adventures 36
    Mahmya Island 36
    St. Shenouda Coptic Orthodox Church 37
    Mini Egypt Park 38
    Sand City Hurghada 38
    Dolphin House 39
    Makadi Bay Water World 39

Chapter 5 41
Accommodation Options 41
    Overview of Accommodation Options 41
    Luxury Hotels 41
    Budget-Friendly Stays 45
    Boutique Guesthouses 48
    Unique Stays (Villas, Apartments) 50

Top Recommended Accommodation 52

Chapter 6 54
Where to Eat in Hurghada 54
Traditional Egyptian Cuisine 54
Best Restaurants for Fine Dining 55
Casual Eateries and Cafés 57
Vegetarian and Vegan-Friendly Spots 59
7.5 Street Food and Markets 60
Top Recommended Restaurants 61

Chapter 7 63
Nightlife in Hurghada 63
Popular Bars and Clubs 63
Live Music Venues 65
Relaxed Evening Spots 67
Safety Tips for Enjoying Nightlife 69

Chapter 8 71
Itineraries for Different Travelers 71
Weekend Getaway (2-3 Days) 71
Cultural Immersion (4-5 Days) 73
Outdoor Adventure (5-7 Days) 74
Family-Friendly Trip (5 Days) 77
Budget Travel (3-5 Days) 79
Solo Traveler's Guide (4-6 Days) 80
Romantic Getaways (3-5 Days) 81

Chapter 9 84
Outdoor Adventures and Nature Activities 84

Diving and Snorkeling 84

Desert Safari and Quad Biking 86

Camel Riding and Bedouin Camps 88

Water Sports (Kitesurfing, Windsurfing) 89

Day Trips to Surrounding Nature Reserves 91

Chapter 10 94
Day Trips from Hurghada 94

Luxor 94

Cairo and the Pyramids 96

El Quseir 97

Safaga 98

Al-Minya 99

Chapter 11 101
Local Culture and Experiences 101

Exploring Hurghada's Markets 101

Art and Museums 103

Local Festivals and Events 105

Shopping for Local Handicrafts and Products 107

Participating in a Traditional Cooking Class 108

Chapter 12 110
Health and Safety Tips 110

Medical Facilities and Clinics in Hurghada 110

Travel Insurance: What to Consider 113

    Staying Safe in Hurghada: General Guidelines 114

    Emergency Numbers and Contact Information 116

Chapter 13 120
What to Do and What Not to Do 120

    Cultural Etiquette 120

    Tipping Guidelines 122

    Respecting Local Customs 123

    Tourist Dos and Don'ts 125

Chapter 14 127
Eco-Friendly Travel in Hurghada 127

    Sustainable Tourism in Hurghada 127

    Choosing Eco-Friendly Tours 129

    Responsible Marine Life and Desert Interactions 131

    Minimizing Your Environmental Footprint 132

Chapter 15 135
Shopping and Markets 135

    Local Markets for Souvenirs 135

    Best Places to Buy Art and Crafts 137

    Supporting Local Businesses 139

Chapter 16 142
Packing Essentials for Hurghada 142

    What to Pack for the Weather 142

    Gear for Water and Desert Activities 144

    Packing for Cultural Activities 145

Travel Insurance and Medical Kit 146

Chapter 17 149
Money and Currency in Hurghada 149
    Using Egyptian Pounds and Payment Options 149
    Credit Card and ATM Access 150
    Tipping and Service Charges 152
    Where to Exchange Money Safely 153

Chapter 18 156
Language and Communication 156
    Arabic Basics for Travelers 156
    Common Phrases You'll Need 158
    English vs. Arabic: Where It's Spoken 159
    Apps and Tools to Help with Translation 161

Chapter 19 164
Practical Travel Tips 164
    Electricity and Plug Types 164
    Internet and SIM Cards 165
    Local Emergency Contacts 167
    Health and Vaccination Requirements 169
    Visa and Entry Requirements for Hurghada 171

Chapter 20 173
Final Thoughts 173
    Making the Most of Your Trip 173
    Must-See Experiences 174

Planning Your Next Visit to Hurghada 176
Encouraging Responsible and Sustainable Travel 178

Chapter 21 180
Appendix 180
Emergency Contacts 180
Maps and Navigational Tools 181
Additional Reading and References 182
Useful Local Phrases 183
Hello: "Salam" (سلام) 183
Addresses and Locations of Popular Accommodation 184
Addresses and Locations of Popular Restaurants and Cafés 185
Addresses and Locations of Popular Bars and Clubs 186
Addresses and Locations of Top Attractions 188
Addresses and Locations of Clinics, Hospitals, and Pharmacies
.... 189
Addresses and Locations of Historical Sites 190

MAPs 192
Map of Hurghada 192
Things to do in Hurghada 193
Hotels in Hurghada 194
Vacation Rentals in Hurghada 195
Restaurants in Hurghada 196
Museums in Hurghada 197
Pharmacies in Hurghada 198
ATMs in Hurghada 199

Hiking Trails in Hurghada	200
IMAGE ATTRIBUTION	201
APPRECIATION	202

Introduction

INTRODUCTION TO HURGHADA

Overview of Hurghada

Hurghada is a resort city in the Red Sea of Egypt, which is famous for its warm climate clean sea and popular among tourists. It used to be a mere fishing station, but over the years it has developed into a city and has become one of the most famous holiday resorts in Egypt. Many visitors arrive to enjoy its white sandy beaches and clear coral reefs as well as the water sports.

Geographically, Hurghada is situated at approximately **27.2579° N latitude and 33.8116° E longitude**, stretching along the coast for over 36 kilometers. There are several key areas to the city. Most of the hotels and restaurants are in **Sekalla** (downtown area), **El Dahar** (old town with local markets and more traditional Egyptian life), and the northern districts that house stunning resorts and new development. Hurghada has a population of around 260,000 with a balance of tourism, local life and growing infrastructure able to accommodate international visitors.

History and Culture of Hurghada

Hurghada's history is relatively recent compared to the ancient wonders found elsewhere in Egypt. Founded as a small fishing village by sea, the place was famed for its calm outlook and abundance of marine life. Until the 20th century though, the town had, for the most part, remained unseen, with a sudden surge of attention due to its close proximity to the Red Sea's crystal clear waters, making it the perfect place for scuba diving and snorkeling. Hurghada's tourism industry began to flourish in the late 1980s and early 1990s and became a world-class destination thereafter.

Culturally, Hurghada has become a melting pot, reflecting the influences of **Egyptian**, **Bedouin**, and **international** lifestyles. The old town, El Dahar, is where you can experience more of the city's traditional side. The streets are lined with souks, mosques and Coptic churches here, with both modern and old-world charm. While most of the city's domestic economy centers on tourism, there is an enduring association with the sea, fishing, and the desert hinterland that surrounds it. Visitors frequently meet friendly locals proud of their Bedouin heritage and tend to share their traditional desert life.

Why Visit Hurghada?

Hurghada is a prime destination for a wide range of travelers. The Red Sea is a diving and snorkeling paradise for the adventure seekers from around the world. Pristine coral reefs and marine life, with brightly **colored fish, dolphins** and even **turtles** are just some of the things that make the area famous. Whether you're an experienced diver or just a beginner, you can find dive schools that offer guided diving at some of the most beautiful underwater spots.

Hurghada is also perfect for families looking for a fun-filled holiday. Its all-inclusive resorts are numerous with water parks, children's clubs and beautiful beaches with safe shallow sea areas for children. For those seeking cultural experiences, trips to nearby cities like Luxor, home to the Valley of the Kings, or Cairo, with its iconic pyramids, are just a day away.

The city also offers a rich desert experience. Adventurous tourists explore the enormous desert terrain as they embark on quad biking, jeep safari, or camel rides; tours include a stop at a Bedouin camp where travelers can experience authentic Egyptian hospitality.

What Makes Hurghada Unique?

The thing that really sets Hurghada apart from Egyptian destinations is its proximity to the Red Sea and the desert. Cities such as Luxor or Cairo have numerous cultural and historical attractions. Still, Hurghada combines this with the natural beauty of the coast and the adventures of the desert.

One of Hurghada's unique features is the Giftun Islands, located just off the coast (latitude 27.2034° N, longitude 33.9581° E). These islands are known for their unspoiled beaches and are a popular destination for day trips, where visitors can enjoy snorkeling in crystal-clear waters teeming with marine life.

In addition to the sea, Hurghada offers visitors the chance to experience Bedouin culture firsthand. The vast desert surrounding the city provides opportunities for desert safaris, where travelers can ride camels, experience a traditional Bedouin meal, and watch the stars in one of the clearest night skies imaginable.

Hurghada's combination of sea, desert, and modern amenities, along with its unique local culture, makes it a diverse and appealing destination for travelers of all kinds.

Chapter 1

HOW TO GET THERE

Nearest Airports

Hurghada International Airport (HRG) is the sole gateway airport for Hurghada, both internationally and also domestically. It is 5 km southwest of the city center at 27.1839° N, 33.7960° E. It's modern and well-equipped, with flights from major aircraft companies from all over the world, including many European flights as well as direct flights from the Middle East and other parts of Egypt.

Cairo International Airport (CAI) is a connecting airport for travelers coming from more remote destinations and Hurghada is about a 1-hour flight away. During the high tourist seasons, the airport has a lot of charter flights, so it's nice for people who want to visit the Red Sea resorts.

Transport Options from the Airport

When you arrive at Hurghada International Airport you have several transport options to get to the city or your accommodation:

Airport Taxis: Taxis are readily available at the airport. While some taxis may not have meters, it's common to negotiate a fixed fare before starting your trip. A typical taxi ride to central Hurghada should cost between 100 and 200 Egyptian pounds, depending on the distance and traffic. It's advisable to use the official airport taxis to avoid being overcharged.

Private Airport Transfers: Many hotels and resorts offer private transfer services for their guests. Pre-arranged can be hassle-free and help you reach your destination. Private transfers which cost depend on distance and vehicle type, are usually more expensive than taxis.

Ride-Hailing Apps: Uber and Careem (a local ride-hailing service) operate in Hurghada, offering an easy and reliable option for getting to your hotel or other destinations. These apps provide transparent pricing and are widely used in the city.

Shuttle Buses: Some tour operators and resorts provide shuttle bus services from the airport. These are generally cheaper than taxis and can be pre-booked or arranged upon arrival.

Traveling by Car: Rentals and Driving Tips

Renting a car in Hurghada is an option for those who prefer flexibility and the ability to explore at their own pace. Car rental services are available both at the airport and throughout the city, with major international companies like Avis, Hertz, and Europcar having offices in the area. Renting a car allows for easy access to nearby attractions like El Gouna or day trips to Luxor.

Driving Tips in Hurghada:

Traffic Rules: Egyptians drive on the right side of the road, and speed limits are typically displayed in kilometers per hour. In Hurghada, the speed limit is generally around 50 km/h in the city and 90-100 km/h on highways.

Road Conditions: Roads in Hurghada are generally well-maintained, but traffic can be unpredictable, especially in busy areas. Be cautious of pedestrians, motorbikes, and the occasional camel crossing!

Parking: Parking is available at most resorts and hotels, often for free. However, finding parking in the downtown areas, particularly in Sekalla, can be challenging during peak times.

Public Transportation Options

While Hurghada is not known for an extensive public transportation system, there are a few local options to get around:

Microbuses: These are the most common form of local transportation in Hurghada. Microbuses are shared minivans that run on set routes around the city. Fares are very inexpensive (usually around 5-10 Egyptian pounds), but routes can be confusing for first-time visitors, and they tend to be crowded. Destinations are often announced by the driver or passengers, so knowing some basic Arabic can be helpful.

Tuk-Tuks: In some parts of Hurghada, especially in local neighborhoods, you may encounter tuk-tuks (small motorized rickshaws). They're an affordable and fun way to travel short distances, though they are less common in tourist-heavy areas.

Buses: While Hurghada does not have a large city bus network, there are intercity buses available for those planning to travel outside Hurghada to cities like Cairo, Luxor, or Alexandria. Companies like Go Bus and Blue Bus operate long-distance routes that are affordable and comfortable.

Ferries: Although not a direct transportation option within Hurghada, the city offers ferry connections to other Red Sea destinations, such as Sharm El-Sheikh. The ferry is a scenic and relaxing way to travel between these cities, with schedules varying by season.

Chapter 2

BEST TIME TO VISIT AND DURATION OF STAY

Hurghada's Climate

The hot summers and mild winters of Hurghada mean it is a suitable year-round destination. It has an average of 365 days of sunshine a year with very little rainfall, often no more than a few millimeters through the year.

Summer (June to August): Temperature can soar to mid-30s and over 40 degrees Celsius in the summertime. The heat may be intense but the coast breeze will help you keep it at a more bearable level. Summer is wonderful because the warm Red Sea waters stay around 26°C to 30°C (79°F to 86°F) so you can participate in water activities like diving and snorkeling.

Winter (December to February): Temperatures are mild, ranging from a high of 17°C/63°F to 22°C/72°F during the day to 10°C/50°F to 13°C/55°F at night in the winter. This makes it a pleasant time to visit for those looking to escape colder climates, though the Red Sea's water temperature drops to around 22°C (72°F), which may be chilly for some swimmers.

Spring (March to May) and Autumn (September to November): These shoulder seasons offer the best balance of warm, pleasant weather with fewer tourists. Spring and autumn temperatures run from 25°C to 30°C (77°F to 86°F), but evenings are cool. During these seasons the temperatures are moderate enough to be spent at the beach or on desert adventures.

Best Seasons to Visit

The best time to visit Hurghada really depends on what type of activities you are going to do. However, **spring (March to May)** and **autumn (September to November)** are often regarded as the most comfortable times of the year to visit, thanks to the moderate weather and fewer tourists.

For Beach and Water Activities: The desert is best explored during winter for quad biking or Bedouin camp visits. Longer excursions can be done without the discomfort of summer heat.

For Desert Adventures: Winter is the best time for exploring the desert, taking a quad biking trip, or visiting Bedouin camps. The mild temperatures allow for longer excursions without the discomfort of the summer heat.

Avoiding Crowds: The peak summer months (July and August) attract large crowds of foreign tourists and locals to the resorts for the summer holidays, so if you are trying to avoid large crowds, you should stay away from these months.

Ideal Duration of Stay for Different Types of Travelers

There is a huge variety of activities and experiences in Hurghada, and this means that the length of stay depends on the type of traveler you are.

Weekend Getaway (2-3 days): For those on a short break, a long weekend is enough to enjoy some of Hurghada's beautiful beaches, take a snorkeling or diving trip, and spend an evening exploring the city's nightlife or visiting the marina.

Relaxation and Beach Holiday (5-7 days): A week in Hurghada, you have plenty of time to go to the beach, to several snorkeling spots, and to chill out at the resorts. You'll also have a chance to take day trips such as a boat trip to the **Giftun** Island or a desert **Safari**.

Adventure Seekers (7-10 days): 7 to 10 days is perfect for travelers who want to dive, kitesurf, and simultaneously explore the desert and the sea. It provides plenty of time for several diving trips, day trips to Luxor and Cairo, or a full day in the desert.

Cultural Explorers (7-10 days): If you are keen on mixing relaxation with culture, then a week or more would be ideal. Then, you get some time to visit some cultural landmarks of the city such as the temples and tomb of Luxor and Hurghada beaches and resorts at the same time.

Special Events and Festivals

Hurghada hosts a number of festivals and events which afford visitors of the opportunity to experience various facets of Egyptian culture and international celebrations.

Hurghada International Festival (February): This annual event includes a series of sporting competitions such as marathons, triathlons, and desert races, attracting participants from around the world. It's a great time to visit if you're a sports enthusiast looking for a lively atmosphere.

Coptic Christmas (January 7th): Celebrated by Egypt's Christian community, Coptic Christmas is an important holiday in Hurghada. Churches host special services, and there is a festive atmosphere in the old town of El Dahar, with street celebrations and traditional foods.

International Camel Race (March): This unique event occurs just outside Hurghada and gives the crowd a chance to see the traditional Bedouin culture. Camel racing is attractive, colorful, and a good memory.

Sham El-Nessim (April): This ancient Egyptian spring festival is celebrated across the country, including Hurghada. Locals head to the beach for picnics and barbecues, and visitors are welcome to join in the festivities. It's a wonderful way to experience local traditions.

Hurghada Summer Festival (July-August): the summer months are the hottest, but the Hurghada Summer Festival is a great way to bring the city to life with concerts, performances and beach parties that attract people from all over.

Chapter 3

TRANSPORTATION WITHIN HURGHADA

Getting Around by Public Transport

Major cities do have a more advanced public transport system, but there is still a way to get around within and out of Hurghada.

Microbuses: Microbuses are the main form of public transport used in Hurghada. Small, shared vans, known as microbuses, run between established routes in the city. Fares are usually between 5 and 10 Egyptian pounds making them affordable and a local way to travel. Popular routes include transport between the El Dahar district and Sekalla, as well as connections to various beaches. Keep in mind that there are no set schedules, and understanding basic Arabic can be helpful to ensure you get off at the right stop.

Taxis: Taxis are also widely available throughout Hurghada. Unlike microbuses, taxis provide direct service and are more comfortable. However, it's important to negotiate the fare before the journey, as most taxis do not have meters. Fares generally range from 20 to 50 Egyptian pounds, depending on the distance. Taxis are a convenient way to reach hotels, beaches, and the marina, though prices can vary during tourist seasons.

Ride-Hailing Services: Uber and Careem, Egypt's leading ride-hailing apps, operate in Hurghada. These apps offer more transparent pricing and are especially useful for tourists who may not be familiar with local rates or Arabic. They are popular for their convenience, especially for airport pickups or traveling between attractions like Hurghada Marina (27.2296° N, 33.8310° E) and your accommodation.

Renting Bicycles and Electric Scooters

For those looking for a more eco-friendly and leisurely way to explore Hurghada, renting bicycles and electric scooters is an increasingly popular option:

Bicycles: Some hotels and resorts offer bicycle rentals, which are great for exploring nearby areas or for short trips along the coast. Hurghada Marina and El Gouna (27.4028° N, 33.6780° E) are particularly bike-friendly, with relatively flat terrain and minimal traffic in certain parts. Prices for bicycle rentals can vary, but they are typically around 100 to 150 Egyptian pounds per day.

Electric Scooters: Electric scooters have become trendy in many parts of Hurghada, particularly among younger tourists. Companies like Scoot-Egypt and other local vendors provide short-term rentals. Scooters are ideal for getting around resort areas or taking short rides to the beach. They offer flexibility without the need to navigate the complexities of public transport. Rental prices usually start at 200 Egyptian pounds per day.

Safety Considerations: Whether you're biking or using an electric scooter, it's important to be cautious, especially in busy areas. Helmets may not always be provided, so it's wise to bring your own if you're planning to rent for multiple days. Also, be aware of local traffic, as Egyptian drivers can be unpredictable.

Local Buses and Shared Taxis

While microbuses are the main form of local shared transport, Hurghada also offers other communal transportation options:

Local Buses: Hurghada has limited local bus routes compared to Cairo or Alexandria, but there are a few options for getting around the city or traveling to nearby destinations. For longer trips, Go Bus and Blue Bus offer intercity routes to cities like Cairo (30.033° N, 31.2333° E) and Luxor (25.7° N, 32.6396° E). These buses are affordable, comfortable, and a reliable alternative to private cars, especially for travelers on a budget.

Shared Taxis: Like most microbuses, shared taxis pick up multiple people and drop them off in various locations. They are smaller than microbuses but provide more direct service, running flexible routes depending on passenger needs. The fare is typically negotiated with the driver, ranging from 10 to 30 Egyptian pounds depending on the distance. Shared taxis are a practical option for trips around popular tourist areas like Sekalla or El Dahar.

Car Rentals and Driving in the City

For visitors who prefer flexibility or are planning day trips outside Hurghada, renting a car can be an ideal solution:

Car Rentals: Hurghada is covered by several international car rental companies, such as **Hertz, Sixt, Europcar**, and some local agencies. The rental costs depend on the kind of vehicle rented and the rental duration: standard cars start from 400 to 700 Egyptian pounds per day. Hurghada International Airport and many other places in the city have car rentals. Those who want to explore more attractions like Makadi Bay (**latitude 26.9908° N, longitude 33.8995° E**) or plan day trips to **El Gouna** will find renting a car very handy.

Driving in Hurghada: Hurghada is a town where driving can be an adventure in itself. The city's roads are in good condition and well-maintained. Drivers should be prepared for traffic patterns and pedestrians crossing at unexpected points. Egyptian drivers tend to be a little more aggressive than the European or even the American standards. Navigation is easy, as helped by road signs in Arabic and English. However, GPS apps like Google Maps or Waze are helpful for finding the best routes.

Parking: Parking in Hurghada is generally easy to find, especially near major resorts, beaches, and tourist attractions. Many hotels and resorts offer free parking for guests, while street parking is often available near local markets and the marina area. Be mindful of designated parking areas to avoid fines, as some parts of the city have parking restrictions.

Chapter 4

TOP 10 TOURIST ATTRACTIONS

Giftun Islands

Coordinates: 27.2154° N, 33.9948° E

This is one of Hurghada's most well-known natural attractions and is best known for its unspoiled beaches and crystal-clear turquoise waters. The islands are a protected marine park, famous for their pristine coral reefs, making them a top destination for snorkeling and diving enthusiasts. Visitors can take day trips to Paradise Island or Orange Bay to enjoy a relaxing day of sunbathing, swimming, and underwater exploration.

Tip: Bring your snorkeling gear to fully enjoy the stunning underwater life around the islands, where you'll see colorful fish, turtles, and occasionally dolphins.

Hurghada Marina

Coordinates: 27.2296° N, 33.8310° E

In the heart of the city is Hurghada Marina, a busy waterfront area featuring some restaurants, bars and shops along its promenade. It is an excellent place to do an evening stroll around the marina, where you get to see luxury yachts and enjoy outstanding international cuisine and breathtaking views of the Red Sea.

Tip: Come to the marina in the evening to see some live music, visit the bars and lounges and enjoy the vibrant evening nightlife scene.

El Gouna

Coordinates: 27.4028° N, 33.6780° E

El Gouna is a resort town located north of Hurghada, known for its luxurious and peaceful lagoons, upscale hotels, and elegant marinas. Known for its eco-friendly design, El Gouna is perfect for travelers looking for a more exclusive and serene experience. The town also offers a wide range of water sports, including kitesurfing and diving, and has an active arts and cultural scene.

Tip: Take a boat ride through the lagoons of El Gouna for a unique way to explore the town and enjoy the stunning views of the Red Sea.

Desert Safari Adventures

Desert safaris are a must for thrill-seekers visiting Hurghada. Guided tours offer exciting activities like quad biking, camel rides, and jeep expeditions through the vast desert. Many desert safaris include a visit to a traditional Bedouin camp, where you can enjoy a meal and experience local Bedouin culture. The adventure often ends with stargazing, offering some of the clearest skies for observing constellations and planets.

Tip: Wear comfortable clothing and bring sunglasses and sunscreen to protect yourself from the desert sun during your safari adventure.

Mahmya Island

Coordinates: 27.1955° N, 33.9772° E

Mahmya Island is an eco-friendly haven within the Giftun Island chain, renowned for its crystal-clear waters and powdery white sand. It's a top destination for snorkeling, allowing visitors to swim with colorful marine life in protected coral reefs. The island's laid-back atmosphere, combined with its beach restaurant serving fresh seafood, makes it the perfect escape for a day trip.

Tip: Book a day trip in advance, as visitor numbers are limited to protect the natural environment. Don't forget your snorkeling gear for an unforgettable underwater experience.

St. Shenouda Coptic Orthodox Church

Coordinates: 27.2579° N, 33.8116° E

Located in the El Dahar district, St. Shenouda Coptic Orthodox Church is an important cultural and religious landmark for Hurghada's Coptic Christian community. The church's beautiful architecture features intricate Coptic designs and icons, making it a peaceful place to explore. It offers a glimpse into the religious diversity and heritage of Egypt, contrasting with the predominantly Islamic culture.

Tip: Attend a Sunday service to experience the local Coptic Christian traditions and see the church in full operation.

Mini Egypt Park

Coordinates: 26.9912° N, 33.8983° E

Located in Makadi Bay, Mini Egypt Park is a fascinating open-air museum featuring scaled-down replicas of Egypt's most famous monuments, such as the Great Pyramids of Giza, the Sphinx, and Abu Simbel. This is an excellent attraction for families and those interested in learning about Egypt's history in a fun and interactive way.

Tip: Take a guided tour to learn more about the history of each monument, or explore the park at your own pace for a more casual experience.

Sand City Hurghada

Coordinates: 27.0587° N, 33.8614° E

Sand City Hurghada is an open-air sand sculpture museum, displaying incredible works of art crafted entirely from sand. The park has two sections: one dedicated to historical figures and another to mythical creatures and fantasy characters. It's a great place to visit with kids, as the sculptures are both impressive and whimsical, making for a fun family outing.

Tip: Visit early in the morning or late in the afternoon to avoid the midday heat while exploring the park.

Dolphin House

Coordinates: 25.6233° N, 34.7853° E

Dolphin House, or Sha'ab Samadai Reef, is one of the best spots in Hurghada to see wild dolphins. The reef, located about 30 kilometers off the coast, is home to a large pod of dolphins that frequent the area. Visitors can join boat trips for a chance to snorkel or dive alongside these majestic creatures, although sightings are never guaranteed, as the dolphins are free to roam.

Tip: Book your Dolphin House trip with a responsible operator who follows ethical guidelines to protect the dolphins and their habitat.

Makadi Bay Water World

Coordinates: 26.9928° N, 33.8983° E

Makadi Bay Water World is a large water park offering over 50 slides and attractions for all ages. From thrilling water slides to relaxing wave pools, it's a great destination for families looking for a fun day out. The park also has dedicated play areas for young children, making it a top choice for families staying in the Makadi Bay area.

Tip: Plan to arrive early to avoid long queues at the slides, especially during peak tourist seasons.

Chapter 5

ACCOMMODATION OPTIONS

Overview of Accommodation Options

With a vast range of accommodation styles, Hurghada suits all tastes and budgets. There are many great choices along the coastline and in the city center, whether you're looking for an all-inclusive luxury resort, a boutique guesthouse, or a budget-friendly stay.

Luxury Hotels

The Oberoi Sahl Hasheesh

Location: 26.9772° N, 33.8988° E

Website: www.oberoihotels.com/hotels-in-sahl-hasheesh-hurghada/

This 5-star luxury resort provides quiet, suite-only rooms, each with an own balcony and some with direct beach access. The hotel has a stunning seaside setting and an exquisite spa that provides treatments including Ayurvedic therapies, massages, and holistic health programs. Guests may enjoy a big outdoor pool with spectacular sea views, gourmet restaurants providing worldwide cuisine, and diving and snorkeling opportunities.

Amenities: Private beach, spa, infinity pool, diving center, gourmet dining, and 24-hour butler service.

Steigenberger ALDAU Beach Hotel

Location: 27.1535° N, 33.8090° E

Website: www.steigenbergeraldauresort.com

This luxury, all-inclusive beachfront resort is ideal for families and guests looking for a complete resort experience. The property includes an 18-hole golf course, a water park with various slides and pools, a private beach, and a diving facility. It also has numerous eating alternatives, ranging from foreign buffets to gourmet dining. Guests may unwind at the spa and wellness center, which features a sauna, steam room, and a variety of treatments.

Amenities: Water park, golf course, private beach, spa, fitness center, children's club, and multiple dining options.

Baron Palace Sahl Hasheesh

Location: 26.9667° N, 33.8975° E

Website: www.baronhotels.com

This luxurious 5-star hotel provides guests with palace-style Accommodation and many rooms with private plunge pools or direct access to the pool. The resort has several swimming pools one of which is an infinity pool for adults only, and several gourmet restaurants. There is a spa with services such as a hammam, sauna, and beauty services, as well as private access to a sandy beach, where tourists can take water sports such as windsurfing or parasailing, among others.

Amenities: Private beach, infinity pools, spa and wellness center, watersports, gourmet dining, and evening entertainment.

Hurghada Marriott Beach Resort

Location: 27.1977° N, 33.8322° E

Website: www.marriott.com/en-us/hotels/hrgsl-hurghada-marriott-beach-resort

This beachfront resort features modern rooms with stunning sea views, private balconies, and direct access to a private beach. The hotel offers multiple dining options, including international buffets, an Italian restaurant, and poolside snacks. It also has a fitness center, tennis courts, and a health club with a sauna and massage treatments. For water sports lovers, the resort provides easy access to diving and snorkeling excursions.

Amenities: Private beach, fitness center, tennis courts, spa services, diving center, and multiple restaurants.

Rixos Premium Magawish Suites & Villas

Location: 27.1681° N, 33.8137° E

Website: www.rixos.com/en/hotel-resort/rixos-premium-magawish-suites-villas

This sprawling all-inclusive resort offers a luxurious range of suites and villas, some of which come with private pools. The resort boasts an extensive aqua park, numerous swimming pools, and direct access to the beach, where guests can enjoy water sports, snorkeling, and diving. The resort also offers several gourmet dining options, a full-service spa, and a fitness center.

Amenities: Private villas with pools, water park, spa, fitness center, private beach, and multiple fine-dining options.

Budget-Friendly Stays

ZYA Regina Resort and Aqua Park

Location: 27.2119° N, 33.8417° E

Website: www.reginaresorthurghada.com

A budget-friendly all-inclusive resort with a private beach, an aqua park, and basic yet comfortable rooms. The hotel provides easy access to Hurghada's main attractions and has several on-site restaurants and bars. It's ideal for families looking for an affordable yet enjoyable stay.

Amenities: Private beach, aqua park, pools, restaurants, and bars.

Elaria Hotel

Location: 27.1976° N, 33.8269° E

Website: www.elariahotel.com

This budget hotel is known for its clean, spacious rooms and convenient location near downtown Hurghada. It offers easy access to local restaurants, shops, and beaches. While the amenities are more basic, guests appreciate the friendly service and comfortable accommodations.

Amenities: Free Wi-Fi, air conditioning, on-site restaurant, and close proximity to beaches.

Sea Garden Hotel

Location: 27.1967° N, 33.8373° E

Website: www.seagarden-hotel.com

A small, family-friendly hotel located near Hurghada's marina, offering simple accommodations with an outdoor pool and restaurant. The hotel is a short walk from the beach and local dining options, making it ideal for budget travelers.

Amenities: Pool, restaurant, proximity to the beach, and family-friendly services.

Royal Star Empire Beach Resort

Location: 27.2122° N, 33.8354° E

Website: www.empirebeachresort.com

This all-inclusive resort provides access to a private beach, several pools, and a variety of dining options. It's ideal for budget-conscious travelers who still want the convenience of all-inclusive amenities.

Amenities: Private beach, pools, all-inclusive dining, and evening entertainment.

Hurghada Dreams Hotel Apartments

Location: 27.2262° N, 33.8365° E

Website: www.hurghadadreamshotel.com

These budget-friendly apartments are ideal for families or long-term visitors, offering spacious rooms with kitchenettes. The property is close to the beach and local attractions, providing a home-like environment for guests. Amenities: Kitchenettes, proximity to the beach, free Wi-Fi, and family-sized apartments.

Boutique Guesthouses

La Maison Bleue El Gouna

Location: 27.4097° N, 33.6782° E

Website: www.lamaisonbleue-eg.com

A beautifully designed European-style mansion offering boutique luxury. The guesthouse has opulent interiors, a private lagoon-side pool, and gourmet dining. Guests can enjoy personalized service and serene surroundings.

Amenities: Private pool, gourmet dining, spa services, and lagoon views.

The Lodge by Quiksilver Boardriders

Location: 27.4096° N, 33.6771° E

Website: www.boardriderselgouna.com

A surf-themed boutique guesthouse located in El Gouna. It offers cozy, stylish rooms and access to the Red Sea's best spots for kitesurfing and other water sports.

Amenities: Surf-themed rooms, access to water sports, and café.

Samra Bay Hotel & Resort

Location: 27.1672° N, 33.8230° E

Website: www.samrabay.com

A small, modern hotel offering chic rooms with direct access to a private beach. The hotel also has a spa and wellness center, making it a perfect boutique option for those seeking a relaxing stay.

Amenities: Private beach, spa, fitness center, and chic design.

Golden Rose Hotel

Location: 27.1975° N, 33.8364° E

Website: www.goldenrosehotel.com

A small guesthouse offering simple accommodations with sea views and rooftop access. It's located near the marina, making it convenient for exploring Hurghada's waterfront area.

Amenities: Rooftop terrace, proximity to the marina, and affordable rates.

Villa Rayan

Location: 27.1896° N, 33.8365° E

Website: www.villarayan.com

A family-run guesthouse with apartment-style accommodations that include kitchen facilities. Perfect for travelers seeking a homey environment.

Amenities: Kitchenettes, family-friendly services, and free Wi-Fi.

Unique Stays (Villas, Apartments)

Villa Shahrazad Hurghada

Location: 27.1835° N, 33.8329° E

Website: www.villashahrazadhurghada.com

This luxurious private villa features traditional Arabian-style architecture, a large garden, and a private pool. Ideal for families or groups looking for a more exclusive stay. Amenities: Private pool, garden, and Arabian-style decor.

El Gouna Villas and Apartments

Location: 27.4028° N, 33.6780° E

Website: www.elgouna.com/accommodation

These private villas and apartments offer lagoon views, modern amenities, and access to El Gouna's various beaches. Ideal for those looking for a home-away-from-home experience.

Amenities: Private pools, lagoon views, and fully equipped kitchens.

Hurghada Comfort Apartments

Location: 27.1963° N, 33.8299° E

Website: www.hurghadacomfort.com

Spacious, modern apartments located close to the beach, providing self-catering options perfect for long-term stays or families.

Amenities: Fully equipped kitchens, free Wi-Fi, and beach access.

Tiba Resort Apartments

Location: 27.2686° N, 33.8365° E

Website: www.tiba-resort.com

A peaceful apartment complex with shared pools and access to recreational facilities. Ideal for those looking for a quiet retreat outside the main city area.

Amenities: Shared pools, recreational facilities, and free Wi-Fi.

Villa 91 Hurghada

Location: 27.1859° N, 33.8243° E

Website: www.villa91hurghada.com

A spacious private villa with a garden, swimming pool, and stylish interiors. This is perfect for families or groups seeking comfort and privacy.

Amenities: Private pool, garden, and fully equipped kitchen.

Top Recommended Accommodation

Based on quality, location, and amenities, here are the top recommendations for Hurghada:

The Oberoi Sahl Hasheesh (Luxury) – www.oberoihotels.com/hotels-in-sahl-hasheesh-hurghada

Steigenberger ALDAU Beach Hotel (Luxury) – www.steigenbergeraldauresort.com

Royal Star Empire Beach Resort (Budget-Friendly) – www.empirebeachresort.com

La Maison Bleue El Gouna (Boutique) – www.lamaisonbleue-eg.com

Villa Shahrazad Hurghada (Unique Stay) – www.villashahrazadhurghada.com

Chapter 6

WHERE TO EAT IN HURGHADA

Traditional Egyptian Cuisine

You're in for a real treat as Hurghada is a melting pot of cultures and you can taste authentic Egyptian cuisine. Koshari (lentils mixed with rice, pasta and chickpeas and covered with a tart tomato sauce), ful medames (fava beans), and molokhia (a soup made from a green herb with chicken or rabbit) are just a few examples of Traditional dishes in Egypt. Seafood is also a major part of Egyptian cuisine, with dishes like grilled fish and shrimp tagine being popular along the coast.

Top Spots for Traditional Egyptian Cuisine:

El Halaka Restaurant

Location: Near the Marina

Website: www.elhalaka.com

This is a local and tourist popular place known for its fresh seafood and traditional Egyptian dishes. You get everything from grilled fish to seafood tagines and a lively atmosphere.

El Dar Darak

Location: 27.1913° N, 33.8408° E

The food at this fabulous restaurant is delicious – Egyptian pies, grilled meats, and seafood. It's cozy atmosphere and local flavor make it a must-try for traditional Egyptian meals.

Star Fish Restaurant

Location: Near the Marina

Website: www.starfishrestaurant.net

Famous for its seafood, Star Fish also offers a range of Egyptian staples such as shish tawook and kofta. It's a great place to sample authentic Egyptian food in a friendly environment.

Best Restaurants for Fine Dining

Hurghada boasts a number of fine dining establishments that offer a mix of international and local flavors. Many of these restaurants are found in luxury resorts or the Marina area, providing exceptional service, gourmet menus, and a refined dining experience.

Top Spots for Fine Dining:

The Grill – Steigenberger ALDAU Beach Hotel

Location: 27.1535° N, 33.8090° E

Website: www.steigenbergeraldauresort.com/dining

A fine dining option specializing in grilled meats and seafood. The Grill is known for its elegant ambiance, outdoor terrace, and views of the Red Sea.

Sky Bar – Kempinski Hotel Soma Bay

Location: 26.8440° N, 33.9928° E

Website: www.kempinski.com/soma-bay/dining

An exclusive rooftop bar and restaurant offering Mediterranean fine dining with breathtaking views. Sky Bar is perfect for a romantic evening or a special celebration.

Little Buddha Hurghada

Location: 27.2067° N, 33.8284° E

Website: www.littlebuddha-hurghada.com

This upscale restaurant and lounge serves gourmet Asian fusion cuisine. The stylish interiors, large sushi menu, and extensive wine list make it one of Hurghada's top fine dining spots.

Casual Eateries and Cafés

For a more relaxed dining experience, Hurghada offers a variety of casual eateries and cafés. These spots are perfect for grabbing a quick bite or enjoying a leisurely meal after a day at the beach.

Top Casual Eateries and Cafés:

The Lodge Restaurant & Bar

Location: Marina Boulevard

Website: www.thelodge-hurghada.com

This casual restaurant offers a mix of international dishes, from pasta and pizza to burgers and salads. With a laid-back vibe and great views of the Marina, it's a popular spot for lunch or dinner.

Retro Pub & Grill

Location: El Kawther District

Website: www.retrohurghada.com

A casual dining spot serving international favorites like steaks, sandwiches, and pizzas. It's a great place to relax with friends, enjoy sports on TV, and have a drink.

Café Moresco

Location: Sheraton Road

A cozy café with a Middle Eastern flair, Café Moresco offers traditional Egyptian coffee, pastries, and small snacks. Perfect for a quick break while exploring Hurghada.

Granada Restaurant & Pub

Location: Dahar District

A casual eatery with a relaxed atmosphere, serving up a mix of Egyptian and international dishes. The outdoor seating makes it a great spot for an evening meal.

Vegetarian and Vegan-Friendly Spots

While Egyptian cuisine traditionally includes a lot of meat and seafood, Hurghada has several restaurants and cafés that cater to vegetarian and vegan diets.

Top Vegetarian and Vegan-Friendly Spots:

Vegetarian House

Location: Near Dahar Market

A small, family-run restaurant that serves vegetarian versions of traditional Egyptian dishes, such as ful medames, falafel, and vegetable tagines. It's a must-visit for plant-based travelers.

The Vegan Lab

Location: Sheraton Road

Hurghada's first 100% vegan restaurant, The Vegan Lab offers plant-based burgers, pizzas, salads, and smoothies. It's a casual, health-conscious spot that's perfect for a quick, delicious meal.

Moby Dick

Location: El Kawther District

Website: www.mobydickhurghada.com

This restaurant offers a wide selection of vegetarian and vegan-friendly options, including salads, vegetable pizzas, and falafel. It's a cozy spot for plant-based diners to enjoy a meal.

Street Food and Markets

Hurghada's bustling markets and street food stalls offer a more authentic and budget-friendly way to sample Egyptian cuisine. Popular street foods include shawarma, falafel, and koshari.

Top Street Food Spots and Markets:

Dahar Market

Location: Dahar District

A bustling market area where you can find vendors selling fresh produce, spices, and delicious street food like falafel wraps, shawarma, and fresh juices. A great place for a quick and inexpensive bite.

Shawarma Station

Location: Sheraton Road

A favorite among locals, this small stall serves up some of the best shawarma in Hurghada. The freshly made wraps are packed with juicy meat, veggies, and tahini sauce.

El Mina Fish Market

Location: Near the Marina

For fresh seafood on the go, El Mina Fish Market offers various street food vendors where you can enjoy fried or grilled seafood while walking around.

Top Recommended Restaurants

Based on quality, service, and food, here are the top recommended restaurants in Hurghada:

El Halaka Restaurant – www.elhalaka.com

Little Buddha Hurghada – www.littlebuddha-hurghada.com

The Grill – Steigenberger ALDAU Beach Hotel – www.steigenbergeraldauresort.com/dining

The Lodge Restaurant & Bar – www.thelodge-hurghada.com

Moby Dick – www.mobydickhurghada.com

Chapter 7

NIGHTLIFE IN HURGHADA

Hurghada offers a lively and varied nightlife scene, ranging from beach bars and nightclubs to live music venues and relaxed lounges. Whether you want to dance the night away or enjoy a quiet drink by the sea, there's something for everyone.

Popular Bars and Clubs

Hurghada's bars and clubs are known for their vibrant atmospheres, international DJs, and beachfront settings. Many of these venues are located around the Marina and in the resort areas, offering stunning views of the Red Sea while you sip cocktails or party into the early hours.

Top Bars and Clubs:

Papas Beach Club

Location: Hurghada Marina

Website: www.papasbeachclub.com

Papas Beach Club is one of Hurghada's most famous nightlife spots, offering beach parties, international DJs, and themed events throughout the year. With a mix of locals and tourists, it's a great place to enjoy a lively night out.

Ministry of Sound Red Sea

Location: Sahl Hasheesh

Website: www.ministryofsound.com

A well-known international brand, the Ministry of Sound Red Sea brings world-class DJs to Hurghada. Located in the luxurious Sahl Hasheesh area, it's the perfect spot for those looking to dance the night away in an upscale atmosphere.

Little Buddha Hurghada

Location: Sheraton Road

Website: www.littlebuddha-hurghada.com

Known for its stylish design and top-tier DJs, Little Buddha is a must-visit for club-goers. The venue features a large dance floor, sushi bar, and a sophisticated cocktail lounge. Its upscale vibe attracts a trendy crowd.

Hed Kandi Beach Bar

Location: Hurghada Marina

With a focus on house music and a chic beachside setting, Hed Kandi Beach Bar offers a more laid-back vibe compared to Hurghada's nightclubs. It's a popular spot for sunset cocktails and pre-party drinks.

Calypso Disco

Location: Sheraton Road

A classic club in Hurghada, Calypso Disco offers a mix of international and local music. With multiple dance floors and live performances, it's a fun and energetic place to party late into the night.

Live Music Venues

For those looking to enjoy live music, Hurghada has several venues that offer everything from local Egyptian bands to international cover artists. Whether you prefer relaxing acoustic sets or lively performances, there are options to suit your taste.

Top Live Music Venues:

Hard Rock Café Hurghada

Location: El Mamsha

Website: www.hardrockcafe.com/location/hurghada

A global icon, Hard Rock Café Hurghada offers live rock music and performances in a lively setting. With American-style dining and a fun atmosphere, it's a great spot for music lovers.

The Heaven Beach Bar & Restaurant

Location: Hurghada Marina

Website: www.heaven-hurghada.com

A relaxed beachfront venue known for its live music and stunning views. The Heaven Beach Bar offers acoustic performances, jazz nights, and themed music events that make for a more chilled-out nightlife experience.

Cadenza Live Music Lounge

Location: Sahl Hasheesh

Website: www.cadenzalivemusic.com

This live music lounge offers intimate performances by local and international artists. The cozy atmosphere and high-quality sound system make it one of the best places in Hurghada for music enthusiasts.

Peanuts Bar – Marriott Hurghada

Location: 27.1977° N, 33.8322° E

Website: www.marriott.com/en-us/hotels/hrgsl-hurghada-marriott-beach-resort

Located inside the Marriott Beach Resort, Peanuts Bar is known for its casual vibe and frequent live music events. With affordable drinks and a laid-back atmosphere, it's a great spot for a night of live entertainment.

Relaxed Evening Spots

For those seeking a more laid-back atmosphere, Hurghada offers plenty of relaxed evening spots. Whether you're looking for a quiet cocktail lounge or a cozy café with sea views, these venues are perfect for unwinding after a busy day of sightseeing.

Top Relaxed Evening Spots:

Moby Dick Restaurant & Lounge

Location: El Kawther District

Website: www.mobydickhurghada.com

Known for its comfortable atmosphere and excellent food, Moby Dick is a great place to enjoy a quiet evening with friends. The lounge area is perfect for sipping cocktails and enjoying a conversation.

White Elephant Thai Restaurant & Lounge

Location: Sahl Hasheesh

Website: www.whiteelephant-thai.com

This stylish Thai restaurant features a relaxed lounge area where you can enjoy drinks in a serene setting. Perfect for those looking for a more tranquil night out.

Wunderbar

Location: Hurghada Marina

A chic cocktail bar located at the Marina, Wunderbar offers a wide selection of drinks and a comfortable atmosphere. It's a popular spot for sunset drinks and casual evening get-togethers.

L'Aubergine Restaurant & Bar

Location: El Gouna

Website: www.laubergine-elgouna.com

This trendy restaurant and bar in El Gouna offers a mix of Mediterranean cuisine and refreshing cocktails. The casual, elegant atmosphere makes it a favorite for relaxed evenings with friends.

El Mashrabeya Roof Bar

Location: Dahar District

This rooftop bar offers beautiful views of the city, making it an ideal place to unwind after a day of exploring Hurghada. The atmosphere is laid-back, and the drinks menu includes both local and international options.

Safety Tips for Enjoying Nightlife

While Hurghada is generally a safe destination, it's important to keep safety in mind when enjoying the nightlife. Here are some tips to ensure a fun and secure night out:

Stay in Groups: It's always safer to go out in groups, especially if you're unfamiliar with the area. Stick with friends and avoid wandering off alone late at night.

Use Trusted Transportation: After a night out, it's best to use reputable taxis, Uber, or Careem for getting back to your hotel. Avoid accepting rides from unregistered taxis or individuals.

Watch Your Drinks: Be mindful of your drinks in bars and clubs. Don't leave them unattended, and always get your drinks directly from the bartender.

Know Local Laws: Be aware of Egypt's laws regarding alcohol consumption. While drinking is permitted in licensed establishments, public drunkenness is frowned upon, and alcohol should not be consumed outside designated areas.

Respect Local Customs: Hurghada is a tourist-friendly destination, but it's still important to respect local customs, especially during religious holidays or in more traditional areas.

Chapter 8

ITINERARIES FOR DIFFERENT TRAVELERS

Hurghada offers a wide range of experiences, making it an excellent destination for various types of travelers. Whether you're visiting for a weekend or looking for a cultural or adventure-filled trip, here are suggested itineraries tailored to different types of visitors.

Weekend Getaway (2-3 Days)

For those short on time, a weekend getaway in Hurghada is perfect for relaxing and soaking up the Red Sea's beauty. Here's a quick itinerary to make the most of your brief visit:

Day 1

Morning: Arrive in Hurghada and head straight to your hotel. After check-in, spend the morning at your resort's beach or pool.

Afternoon: Visit Hurghada Marina for lunch with a sea view at one of the waterfront restaurants. Afterward, take a leisurely walk around the marina and explore its shops.

Evening: Dine at El Halaka Restaurant for a traditional Egyptian seafood experience. End the night with drinks at Papas Beach Club.

Day 2

Morning: Take a half-day boat trip to the Giftun Islands for snorkeling or diving. The crystal-clear waters and vibrant coral reefs make it a must-see destination.

Afternoon: Return to Hurghada and enjoy lunch at your hotel or a café. Spend the rest of the afternoon at your hotel's spa or exploring the local souks.

Evening: Head to Little Buddha Hurghada for a fine dining experience followed by a night of dancing.

Optional Day 3

Morning: Take a short quad biking desert safari in the morning, followed by a relaxing afternoon by the beach.

Afternoon/Evening: Depart from Hurghada.

Cultural Immersion (4-5 Days)

For travelers looking to explore the rich culture and history of the region, this itinerary focuses on local experiences and ancient sites.

Day 1

Morning: Start your day with a visit to St. Shenouda Coptic Orthodox Church to learn about the Coptic Christian community in Egypt.

Afternoon: Head to El Dahar Market, Hurghada's old town, to explore the traditional souks. Try some local street food like koshari or shawarma.

Evening: Enjoy a traditional Egyptian dinner at El Dar Darak.

Day 2

Morning: Take a day trip to Luxor to visit the ancient Valley of the Kings, Karnak Temple, and Hatshepsut Temple.

Afternoon: Explore more of Luxor's heritage sites.

Evening: Return to Hurghada and relax with dinner at The Lodge Restaurant & Bar.

Day 3

Morning: Visit Mini Egypt Park to see miniature versions of Egypt's most famous landmarks, including the Pyramids and the Sphinx.

Afternoon: Spend the afternoon at Hurghada Museum, learning more about the history and archaeology of the Red Sea region.

Evening: Dine at Star Fish Restaurant, known for its local cuisine.

Day 4

Morning: Take a tour of a traditional Bedouin camp in the desert to learn about the nomadic Bedouin culture.

Afternoon: Enjoy a Bedouin-style lunch and explore the desert on camelback.

Evening: Return to Hurghada for a peaceful dinner at Granada Restaurant & Pub.

Outdoor Adventure (5-7 Days)

Hurghada is a paradise for adventure seekers, offering plenty of opportunities for diving, desert safaris, and watersports. Here's a week packed with thrilling activities:

Day 1

Morning: Start your adventure with a diving or snorkeling trip to Dolphin House, where you can swim with dolphins in their natural habitat.

Afternoon: Explore the nearby coral reefs before returning to the marina for lunch.

Evening: Enjoy dinner at The Grill – Steigenberger ALDAU Beach Hotel.

Day 2

Morning: Go kitesurfing at El Gouna, one of the top spots for the sport.

Afternoon: After a full morning of kitesurfing, enjoy lunch at a beachfront café in El Gouna and spend the rest of the day exploring the town.

Evening: Return to Hurghada and relax at Wunderbar for sunset cocktails.

Day 3

Morning: Take a full-day desert safari on quad bikes or dune buggies.

Afternoon: Enjoy a BBQ lunch in the desert before visiting a Bedouin village.

Evening: End the day with stargazing in the desert.

Day 4

Morning: Take a boat trip to Mahmya Island for snorkeling in pristine waters.

Afternoon: Spend the day relaxing on the beach or exploring the island's reefs.

Evening: Return to Hurghada for dinner at The Heaven Beach Bar & Restaurant.

Day 5

Morning: Go horseback riding along the beach or desert trails.

Afternoon: Enjoy some downtime by your hotel pool or visit Makadi Bay Water World for some water park fun.

Evening: End your adventure-packed trip with dinner at Peanuts Bar.

Family-Friendly Trip (5 Days)

Hurghada is an excellent destination for families, with plenty of kid-friendly activities and resorts catering to children.

Day 1

Morning: Arrive in Hurghada and spend the morning getting settled at your family-friendly resort, like Steigenberger Aqua Magic.

Afternoon: Head to the pool or resort's water park for some fun.

Evening: Enjoy a family dinner at Moby Dick Restaurant & Lounge.

Day 2

Morning: Take a family boat trip to Giftun Islands for a day of snorkeling and swimming.

Afternoon: Return to Hurghada and explore the Mini Egypt Park, which kids will love.

Evening: Have dinner at a casual family-friendly restaurant like Retro Pub & Grill.

Day 3

Morning: Spend the day at Makadi Bay Water World, where kids can enjoy various water slides, wave pools, and lazy rivers.

Afternoon: Continue the fun at the water park.

Evening: Relax back at the hotel and have dinner at one of the on-site restaurants.

Day 4

Morning: Visit the Hurghada Grand Aquarium, where kids can learn about marine life and even feed the fish.

Afternoon: Spend some time at the beach, building sandcastles or trying out water sports.

Evening: Enjoy dinner at El Halaka Restaurant, offering both seafood and kid-friendly options.

Day 5

Morning: Take a family-friendly camel ride into the desert for a short safari.

Afternoon: Return to Hurghada for a relaxing afternoon by the pool.

Evening: Wrap up your trip with a relaxed dinner at Granada Restaurant & Pub.

Budget Travel (3-5 Days)

Hurghada is also an excellent destination for budget travelers, with affordable accommodations and plenty of low-cost activities.

Day 1

Morning: Check into a budget hotel like Royal Star Empire Beach Resort.

Afternoon: Spend the afternoon exploring Dahar Market for affordable local food and souvenirs.

Evening: Enjoy dinner at Elaria Hotel's on-site restaurant for an affordable meal.

Day 2

Morning: Head to one of the public beaches, like Old Vic Beach, and spend the day relaxing by the water.

Afternoon: Grab lunch at a local café like Café Moresco.

Evening: Enjoy drinks and a casual dinner at Sea Garden Hotel.

Day 3

Morning: Take a budget-friendly snorkeling tour to nearby coral reefs.

Afternoon: Explore the Hurghada Marina on foot and enjoy lunch at an inexpensive restaurant.

Evening: Relax at your hotel or head to Shawarma Station for a cheap, delicious dinner.

Solo Traveler's Guide (4-6 Days)

Hurghada is a safe and welcoming destination for solo travelers. With friendly locals and plenty of activities, it's easy to meet other travelers or enjoy some solitude.

Day 1

Morning: Check into a solo traveler-friendly hotel like Hurghada Dreams Hotel Apartments.

Afternoon: Take a stroll along Hurghada Marina and stop for lunch at The Lodge Restaurant & Bar.

Evening: Head to Hed Kandi Beach Bar for a relaxed evening with music.

Day 2

Morning: Join a group snorkeling or diving tour to Giftun Islands.

Afternoon: Relax by the beach or pool after your underwater adventure.

Evening: Enjoy dinner at Star Fish Restaurant.

Day 3

Morning: Take a quad biking desert safari, joining other solo travelers.

Afternoon: Visit the Hurghada Grand Aquarium or take a walk through the local souks.

Evening: Enjoy a night out at Papas Beach Club.

Romantic Getaways (3-5 Days)

Hurghada is a great destination for couples looking for a romantic escape. With luxurious resorts, secluded beaches, and candlelit dinners, this itinerary offers a perfect blend of relaxation and romance.

Day 1

Morning: Check into a romantic resort like The Oberoi Sahl Hasheesh.

Afternoon: Spend the afternoon relaxing at the private beach or enjoying spa treatments for couples.

Evening: Have a romantic dinner at The Grill – Steigenberger ALDAU Beach Hotel.

Day 2

Morning: Take a private boat trip to Mahmya Island, where you can snorkel in crystal-clear waters and relax on secluded beaches.

Afternoon: Enjoy a beachside lunch on the island.

Evening: Return to Hurghada for a romantic dinner at Little Buddha Hurghada.

Day 3

Morning: Spend the morning horseback riding on the beach.

Afternoon: Relax at the resort's pool or enjoy a couples' massage at the spa.

Evening: End your trip with a candlelit dinner at Sky Bar – Kempinski Hotel Soma Bay.

Chapter 9

OUTDOOR ADVENTURES AND NATURE ACTIVITIES

Hurghada is known for its thrilling outdoor adventures and access to nature, both in the Red Sea and the surrounding desert. Whether you're diving with colorful marine life, exploring vast desert landscapes, or trying your hand at various water sports, there's plenty of excitement to be found.

Diving and Snorkeling

The Red Sea is one of the world's top diving and snorkeling destinations, and Hurghada offers easy access to vibrant coral reefs and an array of marine life, including dolphins, sea turtles, and tropical fish.

Top Diving and Snorkeling Spots:

Giftun Islands

Coordinates: 27.2154° N, 33.9948° E

A protected marine park with some of the best snorkeling and diving spots near Hurghada. Giftun Islands are home to a variety of colorful coral reefs and an abundance of marine life. Snorkeling tours and diving excursions are available from Hurghada's marina.

Dolphin House (Sha'ab Samadai Reef)

Coordinates: 25.6233° N, 34.7853° E

One of the most popular snorkeling spots where you can swim alongside pods of wild dolphins. Many boat tours offer snorkeling trips to this area, providing opportunities to explore vibrant reefs while respecting the dolphins' natural habitat.

Abu Nuhas Shipwreck

Coordinates: 27.5754° N, 33.9789° E

A well-known diving site for more experienced divers, Abu Nuhas features several shipwrecks lying at shallow depths, making it accessible for divers who want to explore underwater history and marine life.

El Fanadir Reef

Coordinates: 27.1833° N, 33.8833° E

Ideal for both beginners and experienced divers, this reef offers the chance to see moray eels, octopuses, and colorful schools of fish. The calm waters make it perfect for a relaxed diving or snorkeling experience.

Careless Reef

Coordinates: 27.2456° N, 33.8817° E

Another top diving site, Careless Reef is known for its vibrant coral formations and deep drop-offs. It's home to many species of fish, including barracuda and jacks, and is great for underwater photography.

Desert Safari and Quad Biking

The Eastern Desert offers vast, rugged landscapes just waiting to be explored. Desert safaris and quad biking are among the most popular adventure activities in Hurghada, giving travelers the chance to experience the beauty of the desert up close.

Top Desert Safari Adventures:

Quad Biking Safari

Location: Hurghada Desert

Quad biking is one of the most exciting ways to explore the desert. Most tours take you deep into the desert, where you'll ride over sand dunes and visit traditional Bedouin camps. Morning and sunset tours are available, with sunset tours often ending with a BBQ dinner under the stars.

Jeep Safari

Location: Eastern Desert

A jeep safari is a thrilling way to traverse the desert's rugged terrain. Tours typically include visits to Bedouin villages, where you can enjoy tea with the locals, learn about their traditional lifestyle, and even try camel riding.

Sandboarding

Location: Eastern Desert

For those seeking a little more adrenaline, sandboarding is an exciting way to experience the desert. The sand dunes of Hurghada offer the perfect environment for this activity, and many desert tours include it as part of the adventure.

Camel Riding and Bedouin Camps

For a more authentic desert experience, camel riding offers a slower, more traditional way to explore the landscape. Bedouin camps provide a fascinating glimpse into the lifestyle of the desert's nomadic people.

Top Camel Riding and Bedouin Camp Experiences:

Camel Trekking in the Desert

Location: Hurghada Desert

Camel trekking is a peaceful way to explore the desert, and most camel tours end with a visit to a Bedouin camp. These treks can last anywhere from an hour to a full day, depending on the tour.

Bedouin Village Tour

Location: Eastern Desert

Bedouin camps offer visitors the chance to experience traditional Bedouin hospitality. Tours typically include tea, a meal, and storytelling by local Bedouins. You'll learn about Bedouin culture, customs, and survival techniques in the harsh desert environment.

Desert Dinner with Stargazing

Location: Hurghada Desert

Many desert tours offer a traditional Bedouin dinner, complete with authentic Middle Eastern dishes like grilled meats and flatbreads. After dinner, you can enjoy a guided stargazing session in the clear desert sky.

Water Sports (Kitesurfing, Windsurfing)

The steady winds and warm waters of the Red Sea make Hurghada an ideal destination for water sports, particularly kitesurfing and windsurfing. Several schools and rental centers offer lessons for beginners as well as advanced riders.

Top Spots for Water Sports:

El Gouna (Kitesurfing)

Coordinates: 27.4028° N, 33.6780° E

Just north of Hurghada, El Gouna is a hotspot for kitesurfing. The shallow lagoons and constant wind create perfect conditions for the sport. Several kitesurfing schools offer lessons, rentals, and equipment for all levels.

Makadi Bay (Windsurfing)

Coordinates: 26.9908° N, 33.8995° E

A short drive south of Hurghada, Makadi Bay is a popular spot for windsurfing. The calm, warm waters are ideal for beginners, while the more experienced can enjoy the steady winds further offshore.

Soma Bay (Kitesurfing and Windsurfing)

Coordinates: 26.8505° N, 33.9917° E

Soma Bay is another popular destination for water sports enthusiasts. The wide-open spaces and reliable wind make it a favorite for kitesurfers and windsurfers alike. Several water sports centers are located along the bay, offering rentals and lessons.

Hurghada Marina

Coordinates: 27.2296° N, 33.8310° E

For those looking to try something new, the Hurghada Marina offers opportunities for paddleboarding, jet skiing, and parasailing. The calm waters and scenic views of the marina make it a great place for water sports beginners.

Magawish Island

Coordinates: 27.1716° N, 33.8392° E

Magawish Island, located just off the coast of Hurghada, is a hidden gem for water sports. Kitesurfing schools often take trips to the island for more advanced riders looking to practice in unspoiled surroundings.

Day Trips to Surrounding Nature Reserves

Beyond the vibrant waters and desert dunes, Hurghada is also close to several nature reserves that offer unique wildlife experiences and scenic beauty. These reserves are perfect for day trips.

Top Nature Reserves to Visit:

Wadi El-Gemal National Park

Coordinates: 24.5650° N, 35.0892° E

Located south of Hurghada, Wadi El-Gemal National Park is home to diverse wildlife, including wild gazelles and desert foxes. The park also has historical ruins and pristine coral reefs, making it a perfect blend of land and sea exploration.

Gebel Elba National Park

Coordinates: 22.3172° N, 36.3167° E

This remote nature reserve is known for its mountains, mangroves, and unique plant species that can't be found anywhere else in Egypt. A day trip to Gebel Elba offers visitors the chance to explore its rugged terrain and rare wildlife.

Sharm El Naga

Coordinates: 26.9610° N, 33.9094° E

A secluded beach and nature reserve just south of Hurghada, Sharm El Naga is famous for its stunning coral reefs located close to the shore, making it ideal for snorkeling. The calm and shallow waters make it perfect for families or beginners.

Abu Dabbab Bay

Coordinates: 25.3358° N, 34.7363° E

Known for its sea turtles and dugongs, Abu Dabbab Bay is a popular spot for snorkeling and diving. A day trip here offers a chance to swim alongside these gentle creatures while exploring the bay's beautiful coral reefs.

Elba Mountain Desert Reserve

Coordinates: 22.3126° N, 36.3128° E

This lesser-known desert reserve is perfect for those looking to explore the natural beauty of Egypt's desert landscapes. It offers a mix of desert flora, mountain views, and rare wildlife.

Chapter 10

DAY TRIPS FROM HURGHADA

Hurghada serves as an excellent base for exploring some of Egypt's most iconic historical and cultural sites. From ancient temples and tombs to small coastal towns and picturesque nature reserves, these day trips offer a deeper look into the rich history and natural beauty of Egypt.

Luxor

Distance from Hurghada: Approximately 290 km (4 hours by car)

Coordinates: 25.6872° N, 32.6396° E

A day trip to Luxor is a must for history enthusiasts. Luxor, often referred to as the world's greatest open-air museum, is home to some of Egypt's most famous archaeological sites. Split into the East and West Banks of the Nile, Luxor is rich with ancient temples, tombs, and monuments.

Top Attractions in Luxor:

Karnak Temple: The largest temple complex in Egypt, Karnak is a fascinating site that showcases the grandeur of ancient Egyptian architecture and religious devotion.

Valley of the Kings: On the West Bank of Luxor, this necropolis houses the tombs of pharaohs, including the famous tomb of Tutankhamun.

Hatshepsut Temple: This stunning mortuary temple built for Queen Hatshepsut is an architectural masterpiece set against the cliffs of Deir el-Bahari.

Luxor Temple: Located in the heart of the city, Luxor Temple is another significant monument with massive statues and grand columns.

How to Get There:

Luxor can be reached by car (approximately 4 hours) or through organized tours that include transportation. Some tours offer private vehicles for a more comfortable trip. If you want to explore more in Luxor, an overnight stay is recommended.

Cairo and the Pyramids

Distance from Hurghada: Approximately 450 km (5-6 hours by car)

Coordinates: 30.0331° N, 31.2334° E

A day trip to Cairo gives you the chance to explore Egypt's bustling capital city and see the world-famous Pyramids of Giza. While it's a long journey from Hurghada, visiting Cairo and the Pyramids is worth the effort for those fascinated by ancient history.

Top Attractions in Cairo:

Pyramids of Giza and the Sphinx: These iconic structures, dating back over 4,000 years, are among the Seven Wonders of the Ancient World and are a must-visit for anyone interested in Egypt's ancient history.

The Egyptian Museum: Home to thousands of ancient artifacts, including the treasures of Tutankhamun, this museum offers an incredible glimpse into Egypt's rich history.

Khan El Khalili Bazaar: After visiting the pyramids, spend some time exploring this bustling market, known for its handcrafted goods, spices, and souvenirs.

How to Get There:

Cairo can be reached by car (5-6 hours) or by plane (about 1 hour). Many tour companies in Hurghada offer day trips by bus or private car, often including stops at the Pyramids and the Egyptian Museum.

El Quseir

Distance from Hurghada: Approximately 140 km (2 hours by car)

Coordinates: 26.1055° N, 34.2779° E

El Quseir is a historic coastal town that offers a more relaxed and culturally rich experience. Known for its ancient trading port, charming old town, and beautiful coral reefs, El Quseir is an excellent day trip for those looking to explore a quieter side of Egypt.

Top Attractions in El Quseir:

Ottoman Fort: This historic fort offers panoramic views of the town and the Red Sea. It also houses a small museum detailing the history of El Quseir.

Old Town: Wander through the narrow streets of the old town to discover traditional homes and local markets.

Diving and Snorkeling: El Quseir is known for its pristine coral reefs, making it a great destination for snorkeling and diving enthusiasts.

How to Get There:

El Quseir is a 2-hour drive from Hurghada. It's easily accessible by car, and many hotels in Hurghada can arrange day trips to the town.

Safaga

Distance from Hurghada: Approximately 60 km (1 hour by car)

Coordinates: 26.7512° N, 33.9368° E

Safaga is a small port town known for its clear waters, unspoiled beaches, and excellent windsurfing and kitesurfing conditions. While less well-known than Hurghada, Safaga is a fantastic destination for water sports and relaxation by the sea.

Top Attractions in Safaga:

Windsurfing and Kitesurfing: Safaga is one of the best spots for windsurfing and kitesurfing on the Red Sea, thanks to its consistent winds and calm waters. Several water sports centers offer lessons and equipment rentals.

Coral Reefs: The reefs around Safaga are home to colorful marine life, making it an excellent spot for snorkeling and diving.

Mineral-Rich Beaches: Safaga's beaches are said to have therapeutic benefits due to their high mineral content, particularly for those suffering from skin conditions.

How to Get There:

Safaga is only about an hour's drive from Hurghada, making it one of the easiest day trips. It's a popular destination for both organized tours and self-drive day trips.

Al-Minya

Distance from Hurghada: Approximately 410 km (5-6 hours by car)

Coordinates: 28.0914° N, 30.7618° E

Al-Minya, located in Middle Egypt, is an off-the-beaten-path destination that offers visitors the chance to explore lesser-known ancient sites. It's a culturally rich area with stunning historical landmarks dating back to the Pharaonic, Greco-Roman, and early Christian eras.

Top Attractions in Al-Minya:

Beni Hassan Tombs: These ancient tombs date back to the Middle Kingdom of Egypt and feature incredibly well-preserved murals depicting scenes of daily life.

Tell el-Amarna: The remains of the city built by the pharaoh Akhenaten, who famously worshipped the sun god Aten. Tell el-Amarna offers a unique insight into a short-lived chapter of Egyptian history.

Tuna el-Gebel: A vast necropolis where you'll find ancient tombs and catacombs. The site is famous for its burial chambers dedicated to the god Thoth and its beautifully decorated tombs.

How to Get There:

Al-Minya is about a 5-6 hour drive from Hurghada. While it's farther than some of the other day trips, organized tours make it possible to visit key archaeological sites in a day. Alternatively, you may consider spending a night in Al-Minya for a more relaxed visit.

Chapter 11

LOCAL CULTURE AND EXPERIENCES

Hurghada is more than just a beach destination; it also offers a glimpse into Egyptian culture, local traditions, and vibrant markets. From art galleries to cooking classes, there are plenty of ways to immerse yourself in Hurghada's cultural experiences.

Exploring Hurghada's Markets

The markets of Hurghada offer a vibrant and bustling atmosphere, where you can experience the local way of life. The souks and bazaars are filled with colorful stalls selling everything from spices and textiles to fresh produce and traditional crafts.

Top Markets in Hurghada:

El Dahar Souk (Old Market)

Location: El Dahar District

This traditional market is one of the best places to experience authentic Egyptian shopping. Stalls are packed with spices, herbs, fruits, vegetables, clothing, and souvenirs. Haggling is expected here, so be prepared to negotiate prices. It's a great spot to buy shawls, scarves, and handcrafted goods.

Hurghada Fish Market

Location: Near the Marina

For those interested in the local seafood scene, Hurghada's fish market offers a lively and authentic experience. You can see a wide variety of fresh seafood brought in by local fishermen and sample dishes at nearby seafood stalls.

Sheraton Road Shopping Area

Location: Sheraton Road

While this area is more tourist-oriented, you'll find a mix of shops offering local products like leather goods, jewelry, and souvenirs, as well as Egyptian cotton items.

Tip: Visit the markets in the morning or late afternoon to avoid the midday heat and ensure you get the freshest produce.

Art and Museums

Hurghada may not be as well-known for its art and museums as Cairo or Luxor, but it still offers several opportunities to explore Egyptian history and creativity. From modern galleries to archaeological collections, there's something for everyone interested in the arts.

Top Art and Museum Experiences:

Hurghada Museum

Location: Village Road

Opened in 2020, Hurghada Museum showcases over 1,000 artifacts from ancient Egypt, highlighting the country's vast history. The museum's displays range from pharaonic statues to Coptic and Islamic art. It's an excellent way to learn about Egypt's cultural heritage in a modern setting.

Sand City Hurghada

Location: Near Senzo Mall

This unique open-air museum features incredible sculptures made entirely out of sand. There are two sections: one dedicated to historical figures and another to fantasy characters. Sand City is a family-friendly attraction and a fun way to appreciate artistic craftsmanship.

Mini Egypt Park

Location: Makadi Bay

While not an art gallery, Mini Egypt Park offers an artistic take on Egypt's most famous landmarks in miniature form. Explore the Pyramids of Giza, Abu Simbel, and Karnak Temple, all in one place.

Website: www.miniegyptpark.com

Contemporary Art Gallery El Gouna

Location: El Gouna

For a more modern experience, head to El Gouna's Contemporary Art Gallery. It features works by both Egyptian and international artists, ranging from paintings and sculptures to photography. It's a great spot for art lovers and collectors.

Website: www.artgalleryelgouna.com

Local Festivals and Events

Hurghada hosts several festivals and cultural events throughout the year, offering visitors a chance to experience Egyptian traditions and local celebrations. From religious festivals to sports events, there's always something happening in this lively city.

Top Festivals and Events:

Hurghada International Festival

When: February

This annual event includes sporting competitions like marathons, triathlons, and desert races, attracting athletes from all over the world. There are also cultural activities, music performances, and local vendors offering food and crafts.

Sham El-Nessim (Spring Festival)

When: April (on the Monday after Coptic Easter)

An ancient Egyptian festival that marks the beginning of spring, Sham El-Nessim is celebrated with picnics, outdoor activities, and traditional Egyptian foods. Locals and tourists alike head to Hurghada's beaches for family gatherings, making it a festive and colorful time to visit.

Coptic Christmas

When: January 7th

While Christmas is celebrated on December 25th around the world, Egypt's Coptic Christians celebrate on January 7th. It's a religious holiday with special church services at places like St. Shenouda Coptic Orthodox Church, and the streets are filled with festive lights and decorations.

Hurghada Summer Festival

When: July-August

The Hurghada Summer Festival brings together music, performances, and beach parties during the hottest months of the year. With live DJ sets and international artists, it's a lively time to experience Hurghada's vibrant nightlife scene.

Shopping for Local Handicrafts and Products

Hurghada's markets and shops are full of local handicrafts and products that make for great souvenirs. From handmade textiles to traditional jewelry, you'll find plenty of unique items that reflect Egypt's rich culture.

Top Handicrafts and Souvenirs:

Alabaster and Stone Carvings: Alabaster is a beautiful stone used to create small statues, bowls, and decorative items. Many shops in Hurghada offer hand-carved alabaster products inspired by ancient Egyptian designs.

Handwoven Rugs and Carpets: You'll find beautiful handwoven rugs and carpets in Hurghada's markets, made by local artisans using traditional techniques. These colorful pieces make for unique and practical souvenirs.

Egyptian Cotton: Renowned for its high quality, Egyptian cotton products such as towels, scarves, and bed linens are available in Hurghada's shops. Look for cotton items in markets or specialized shops along Sheraton Road.

Jewelry: Silver jewelry is particularly popular in Egypt, often featuring scarab beetle designs, Ankh symbols, or other traditional motifs. Many shops offer hand-crafted pieces made from silver or gold, as well as gemstones.

Papyrus Paintings: Papyrus, the ancient paper used by the Egyptians, is still made and sold in Hurghada today. You can buy beautifully painted pieces depicting scenes from Egyptian mythology and history.

Participating in a Traditional Cooking Class

One of the best ways to immerse yourself in Egyptian culture is by learning how to cook traditional dishes. Several cooking schools and local chefs offer classes that allow visitors to experience the rich flavors and techniques of Egyptian cuisine firsthand.

Top Cooking Class Experiences:

Egyptian Cooking Class at El Gouna

Location: El Gouna

This hands-on class takes place in a local chef's home, where participants learn to prepare traditional

Egyptian dishes such as koshari, stuffed grape leaves, and molokhia. After cooking, guests enjoy the meal they've prepared together.

Cooking with a Local Family

Location: Hurghada Old Town

Experience a day with a local family as they guide you through the preparation of a classic Egyptian meal. You'll learn how to make staples like falafel, foul medames, and Egyptian bread, while also getting a glimpse of local life.

Red Sea Fish Cooking Class

Location: Near the Marina

Learn how to cook the fresh catch of the day from Hurghada's vibrant fish market. This cooking class focuses on seafood dishes, teaching participants how to prepare fish using traditional Egyptian spices and techniques.

Chapter 12

HEALTH AND SAFETY TIPS

Safety is essential while on vacation, and traveling to Hurghada means you need to have your health and safety priorities well sorted. While talking about these tips, you will learn how to find medical facilities, what you need to know about local customs and emergency numbers you may need during the trip.

Medical Facilities and Clinics in Hurghada

Hurghada has several high-quality medical facilities and clinics catering to both locals and tourists. Most of these facilities provide general and emergency services, consultation, and special services. Some clinics offer the services of multilingual staff particularly when attending to foreigners or international patients.

Top Medical Facilities in Hurghada:

El Gouna Hospital

Location: El Gouna

Website: www.elgounahospital.com

El Gouna Hospital is among the leading private hospitals in the Hurghada area providing emergency, surgical and other Essential services, other services include orthopedic services and internal medicine. This is well-equipped and all the staff can speak English and that makes it most appropriate for foreigners.

Nile Hospital Hurghada

Location: Sheraton Road

Website: www.nilehospitalhurghada.com

Nile Hospital offers 24-hour emergency care, in addition to general medical services and specialist consultations in areas such as cardiology, pediatrics, and dermatology. It is centrally located and easily accessible for tourists.

Red Sea Hospital

Location: Near the Airport Road

Website: www.redseahospital.com

This modern hospital is known for its emergency services and surgical departments. It caters to tourists and expatriates in Hurghada and offers multilingual staff for easier communication.

German Medical Clinic

Location: El Kawther District

Website: www.gmc-hurghada.com

This private clinic provides a wide range of medical services, including general consultations, laboratory diagnostics, and physiotherapy. It is well-regarded for its high standards of care and experienced medical staff.

Hurghada Hospital

Location: Dahar District

Hurghada Hospital is a public medical facility that offers basic healthcare services and emergency care. It is primarily used by locals but is available to tourists in case of an emergency.

Tip: Always carry your travel insurance details and identification with you in case you need medical assistance. Most private hospitals and clinics in Hurghada accept international insurance or provide receipts for reimbursement.

Travel Insurance: What to Consider

Travel insurance is essential when visiting Hurghada, as it can cover unexpected medical expenses, trip cancellations, and other emergencies. Here are a few things to keep in mind when choosing your insurance policy:

Key Considerations for Travel Insurance

Medical Coverage: Ensure your insurance policy covers emergency medical treatment, hospital stays, and any potential medical evacuations. Check if it includes coverage for common adventure activities in Hurghada, such as diving, snorkeling, or desert safaris.

Trip Cancellation/Interruption: Look for policies that protect against trip cancellations or interruptions due to illness, accidents, or other unforeseen events.

Lost or Stolen Items: Some insurance plans cover lost or stolen luggage, passports, or personal items. This can be helpful if you plan on bringing valuable items with you.

Activity-Specific Coverage: If you're planning on diving, windsurfing, or quad biking, make sure your insurance policy covers these activities, as some may be excluded from standard coverage.

24/7 Assistance: Choose an insurance provider that offers 24/7 assistance, so you can easily access help in case of an emergency.

Tip: Keep a digital copy of your travel insurance policy on your phone or email, along with the contact details for the insurance company's emergency line.

Staying Safe in Hurghada: General Guidelines

Hurghada is generally a safe destination, but like anywhere, it's important to take precautions to ensure your safety. Following these general safety guidelines can help you stay secure during your trip.

General Safety Tips

Stay Hydrated and Protect Yourself from the Sun: The desert climate can be extremely hot, especially in the summer. Drink plenty of water, wear sunscreen, and use protective clothing, such as hats and sunglasses, to avoid sunburn and heatstroke.

Use Reputable Transportation: Stick to trusted taxis, ride-sharing apps like Uber or Careem, or private car services offered by your hotel. Avoid accepting rides from unofficial taxis or strangers.

Avoid Walking Alone at Night: While Hurghada is generally safe, it's best to avoid walking alone late at night, especially in less-populated areas. Stick to well-lit, busy streets and travel in groups when possible.

Be Aware of Scams: Like in many tourist destinations, petty scams and overcharging can happen. Be cautious when approached by overly friendly strangers offering deals, and always agree on a price before taking a taxi or engaging in any service.

Respect Local Customs: Egypt is a conservative country, so it's important to respect local customs and dress modestly, especially when visiting religious sites or rural areas. Public displays of affection should be kept to a minimum, and alcohol consumption is only permitted in licensed establishments.

Street Food Safety: If you want to try local street food, make sure to choose vendors with a high turnover of customers. This ensures that the food is fresh. Avoid drinking tap water and opt for bottled water instead.

Marine Safety: Be cautious when swimming or snorkeling in the Red Sea. Pay attention to local warnings about strong currents or dangerous marine life, such as jellyfish or lionfish. Never touch coral reefs, as they can be sharp and damaging to marine ecosystems.

Emergency Numbers and Contact Information

It's important to know who to contact in case of an emergency while in Hurghada. Keep these emergency numbers and contact details saved on your phone and accessible during your trip.

Key Emergency Numbers in Hurghada:

Ambulance: 123

Police: 122

Fire Department: 180

Tourist Police: 126

The Tourist Police are available to assist with any issues involving tourists, including theft, lost passports, or harassment.

Useful Contact Information

Hurghada International Airport:

Phone: +20 65 344 2590

Website: www.hurghada-airport.co

Embassies and Consulates:

British Embassy in Cairo (Consular services in Hurghada):

Phone: +20 2 2791 6000

Website: www.gov.uk/world/organisations/british-embassy-cairo

U.S. Embassy in Cairo (Consular services in Hurghada):

Phone: +20 2 2797 3300

Website: www.usembassy.gov

German Embassy in Cairo:

Phone: +20 2 2728 2000

Website: kairo.diplo.de

Local Hospitals and Clinics

El Gouna Hospital

Phone: +20 65 358 0011

Website: www.elgounahospital.com

Nile Hospital Hurghada

Phone: +20 65 346 0000

Website: www.nilehospitalhurghada.com

Red Sea Hospital

Phone: +20 65 344 5701

Website: www.redseahospital.com

Tip: For non-emergency medical advice or general inquiries, your hotel reception can often recommend trusted local doctors or clinics.

Chapter 13

WHAT TO DO AND WHAT NOT TO DO

When traveling to a new destination, we must start learning about and respecting the local culture, customs, and social norms. While Hurghada is a tourist-friendly city, it is still a conservative country, so understanding and observing some cultural rules will help you get the most out of your visit but in the right way.

Cultural Etiquette

Understanding Egyptian cultural norms will help you blend in and show respect for the local way of life. Though Hurghada, unlike other parts of Egypt, is much more liberal because of its huge number of international tourists, it is essential to be careful about traditions.

Key Points of Cultural Etiquette

Greetings: Egyptians are nice people who are usually welcoming. When meeting someone, greet them with a warm smile and a "Salam Alaikum" (Peace be upon you). The traditional response is "Wa Alaikum Salam" (And peace be upon you). Handshakes are common, but women may prefer not to shake hands with men—wait for a cue.

Public Displays of Affection: PDA should be kept to a minimum in public spaces. While hand-holding between couples is generally accepted in tourist areas, anything more intimate is considered inappropriate in public.

Dress Modestly: Although you'll see tourists in swimwear at the beach and hotel pool, it's best to dress modestly in public places like markets, malls or restaurants. If women are visiting religious sites or local neighborhoods, they are encouraged to wear clothing that covers the shoulders and the knees. Walking shirtless also shouldn't be done by men in public spaces.

Entering Religious Sites: When you visit mosques or churches, wear appropriate clothes. A scarf over the hair, along with shoulders and legs covered, is what women should wear. Men should avoid shorts. When entering a mosque, always remove your shoes.

Tipping Guidelines

Tipping (known as "baksheesh") is a common and expected practice in Egypt, and Hurghada is no exception. Tipping is not required, but it's an excellent way to show appreciation for good service and provides a meaningful supplemental source of income for many service workers.

Tipping Guidelines

Restaurants and Cafés: It's customary to tip 10-15% in restaurants, even if a service charge is already included in the bill. The service charge typically goes to the restaurant, not the staff, so leaving a small tip directly for the server is appreciated.

Hotels: Tip the porter or bellhop 10-20 EGP for carrying your bags to your room. Housekeeping staff generally receive 20-30 EGP per day, which can be left in your room when you check out.

Taxi Drivers: It's common to round up the fare to the nearest 5 or 10 EGP when using a taxi. For longer trips, a tip of 10-20 EGP is appropriate if the driver has been helpful.

Tour Guides: For day trips and excursions, tipping your guide is customary. A tip of 50-100 EGP per person, depending on the length of the tour, is a good guideline. You can also tip drivers 20-50 EGP depending on the service.

Bathroom Attendants: Public restrooms often have attendants who keep them clean, and it's customary to leave a small tip (around 1-2 EGP) after using the facilities.

Tip: Always carry small bills in Egyptian pounds (EGP) for tipping, as it's easier and more convenient for locals to accept tips in the local currency.

Respecting Local Customs

Hurghada may have a more relaxed atmosphere than other parts of Egypt, but respecting local customs is important, especially when you venture into more traditional areas or visit cultural landmarks.

Key Local Customs to Respect

Ramadan: During the holy month of Ramadan, Muslims fast from dawn to sunset. While tourists are not expected to fast, it's respectful to avoid eating, drinking, or smoking in public during daylight hours, especially in more local neighborhoods. Many restaurants cater to tourists and will still serve food, but be mindful of those fasting.

Alcohol Consumption: Alcohol is available in tourist areas, hotels, and restaurants, but public drunkenness is considered disrespectful. It's best to limit alcohol consumption to licensed establishments and avoid drinking in public spaces.

Photography: Always ask for permission before taking photos of locals, especially women. In some religious sites, photography may be restricted, so be sure to check before snapping photos. Avoid taking photos of military or government buildings, as this is strictly prohibited.

Gender Roles: Egypt is a conservative country, and interactions between men and women may be more formal than what tourists are used to. For example, avoid overly familiar behavior with locals of the opposite gender. It's also customary for men to greet men and women to greet women first, so follow the lead of locals in mixed-gender interactions.

Tourist Dos and Don'ts

To ensure you have a smooth and enjoyable trip in Hurghada, it's helpful to follow these general dos and don'ts when traveling through the city and interacting with locals.

Tourist Dos

Do Respect the Dress Code: While beaches and resort areas are more relaxed, it's important to dress modestly when exploring markets, religious sites, and local neighborhoods.

Do Learn Basic Arabic Phrases: Learning a few Arabic phrases, such as "Shukran" (thank you) and "Afwan" (you're welcome), will go a long way in showing respect and appreciation for local culture.

Do Be Patient When Haggling: Bargaining is expected in many of Hurghada's markets and shops, but it's important to do so with patience and a friendly attitude. Haggling is part of the local culture, and it's more about the experience than the outcome.

Do Drink Bottled Water: The tap water in Hurghada is not safe for drinking. Always opt for bottled water, which is readily available in shops and hotels.

Tourist Don'ts

Don't Display Affection Publicly: Keep public displays of affection, such as kissing or hugging, to a minimum, as they are considered inappropriate in Egyptian culture.

Don't Show Disrespect to Religion: Egypt is a deeply religious country, and showing disrespect to Islam or other religions, whether through words, actions, or jokes, is considered highly offensive.

Don't Give Money to Begging Children: While it may be tempting to give money to children who beg, it's best to avoid doing so, as this can perpetuate the problem. Instead, consider donating to local charities that work to support children and families in need.

Don't Use Your Left Hand: In many Middle Eastern cultures, including Egypt, the left hand is considered unclean. Avoid using your left hand to eat, give money, or shake hands.

Chapter 14

ECO-FRIENDLY TRAVEL IN HURGHADA

As tourism continues to grow in Hurghada, it's important to ensure that your travels have a positive impact on the environment and local communities. By choosing eco-friendly options and being mindful of your activities, you can help preserve Hurghada's natural beauty and cultural heritage for future generations. This chapter offers practical tips for sustainable travel in Hurghada.

Sustainable Tourism in Hurghada

Sustainable tourism in Hurghada involves supporting local communities, protecting natural resources, and minimizing your impact on the environment. As more visitors discover Hurghada's pristine beaches, coral reefs, and deserts, there is growing awareness of the need to protect these natural wonders.

Ways to Support Sustainable Tourism:

Stay in Eco-Friendly Accommodations: Many hotels and resorts in Hurghada are adopting sustainable practices such as reducing energy consumption, minimizing waste, and using eco-friendly materials. Look for accommodations that have sustainability certifications or focus on green initiatives like water conservation and waste reduction.

Examples:

Steigenberger ALDAU Beach Hotel: Known for its eco-friendly initiatives, including energy efficiency and waste reduction.

The Oberoi Sahl Hasheesh: This resort emphasizes eco-conscious operations, such as using solar energy and sustainable water management.

Support Local Businesses: By shopping at local markets, eating at locally-owned restaurants, and using local guides, you contribute to the economic well-being of the community and reduce the carbon footprint associated with imported goods and services.

Respect Natural Resources: Whether you're on a diving tour or exploring the desert, always follow guidelines that protect the environment. Avoid touching coral reefs, leave natural areas as you found them, and never litter in public spaces.

Choosing Eco-Friendly Tours

Many tour operators in Hurghada are now offering eco-friendly tours that prioritize sustainability, responsible travel practices, and environmental protection. Choosing the right tour operator can help ensure your excursions have a positive impact on the environment.

How to Choose Eco-Friendly Tours

Look for Sustainable Certifications: Choose tour operators that are certified by recognized eco-tourism organizations. Certifications indicate that the company adheres to responsible tourism practices, such as minimizing waste and respecting wildlife.

Ask About the Environmental Impact: Before booking a tour, ask how the company minimizes its environmental footprint. For example, some operators use electric boats to reduce water pollution, or offer group tours to reduce the carbon emissions from transportation.

Choose Smaller Groups: Eco-friendly tours often limit the number of participants to reduce their environmental impact. Smaller groups are also less likely to disturb wildlife and cause damage to sensitive ecosystems.

Examples of Eco-Friendly Tours:

Eco-Diving and Snorkeling Tours

Many diving companies in Hurghada, such as Red Sea Diving Safari, follow strict eco-friendly guidelines, including respecting marine life, using environmentally friendly products on board, and organizing beach and reef clean-ups.

Desert Eco-Safari

Some desert tour operators, like Bedouin Eco-Tours, offer environmentally conscious desert safaris that include education on local ecosystems, respect for Bedouin traditions, and minimal use of motorized vehicles to reduce pollution.

Wildlife Conservation Tours

Tours like Hurghada Dolphin Eco-Tours focus on responsible dolphin-watching and marine life interactions. These tours follow strict rules to ensure that marine animals are not disturbed or harmed.

Responsible Marine Life and Desert Interactions

Hurghada's natural landscapes, including the Red Sea and the surrounding deserts, are home to a wide variety of wildlife. While exploring these environments, it's important to interact responsibly to avoid harming fragile ecosystems.

Guidelines for Responsible Marine Life Interactions

Don't Touch Coral Reefs or Marine Animals: Coral reefs are incredibly fragile and can be easily damaged by human touch. Similarly, while snorkeling or diving, never touch or feed marine animals, as this can disrupt their natural behavior and damage the ecosystem.

Avoid Using Harmful Sunscreens: Some sunscreens contain chemicals that can damage coral reefs and marine life. Opt for reef-safe sunscreens that are free from harmful ingredients like oxybenzone and octinoxate.

Respect Marine Life: If you're participating in activities like dolphin-watching, always maintain a safe distance and avoid chasing or disturbing the animals. Choose ethical tour operators that follow guidelines to protect marine species.

Guidelines for Responsible Desert Interactions

Stick to Established Paths: When exploring the desert on foot or by vehicle, stay on designated trails to avoid damaging fragile desert ecosystems. Off-roading can disrupt local wildlife habitats and cause long-lasting environmental damage.

Respect Bedouin Culture: Many desert tours include visits to Bedouin villages. It's important to interact with Bedouins in a respectful manner, by following cultural norms and supporting their sustainable lifestyle through responsible tourism.

Leave No Trace: Whether you're hiking, camping, or on a safari, always clean up after yourself. Take all trash with you and avoid leaving behind any materials that could harm the environment.

Minimizing Your Environmental Footprint

Reducing your environmental impact while traveling is key to sustainable tourism. Here are some practical tips to help you minimize your environmental footprint while exploring Hurghada.

Tips for Reducing Your Impact

Limit Plastic Use: Bring a reusable water bottle, as plastic waste is a major environmental issue in Egypt. Many hotels offer filtered water stations where you can refill your bottle. Avoid using plastic bags and opt for reusable shopping bags when visiting markets or shops.

Conserve Water and Energy: Hotels in Hurghada often use large amounts of water and energy to maintain their facilities. Be mindful of your water usage by taking shorter showers and reusing towels. Turn off lights and air conditioning when leaving your room to conserve energy.

Choose Sustainable Transportation: Opt for eco-friendly transportation whenever possible. Use bicycles or walk when exploring nearby attractions. For longer trips, consider carpooling or using ride-sharing services like Uber or Careem to reduce your carbon footprint.

Respect Wildlife and Nature: Avoid purchasing products made from endangered species or plants, such as coral jewelry or tortoiseshell. These items are often harvested illegally and contribute to the destruction of ecosystems.

Support Conservation Initiatives: Many organizations in Hurghada focus on marine conservation and environmental protection. Consider donating to or volunteering with local environmental groups that work to protect the Red Sea's delicate ecosystems.

Chapter 15

SHOPPING AND MARKETS

There are several charming markets, shops, and kiosks selling souvenirs, handmade crafts, and products made in Hurghada. Whether you prefer a traditional market selling toys or a contemporary enclosed shopping center selling everything you can imagine, this chapter will help you uncover the most fulfilling shopping destinations while empowering the local economy.

Local Markets for Souvenirs

One of the most exciting things when shopping in Hurghada is visiting the numerous local markets called "souks" because they showcase many products and souvenirs of Egyptian origin. These markets are packed with fruit stalls, clothes shops, souvenir stalls, spices shops, handcrafted items, and many more.

Top Local Markets for Souvenirs

El Dahar Souk (Old Market)

Location: El Dahar District

One of the most well-known markets in Hurghada is El Dahar Souk. This is the best place to shop for local products such as scarves, shawls, ornaments and spices. You'll also find a variety of local crafts, such as alabaster figurines, leather goods, and handmade pottery. Haggling is common here, so be prepared to negotiate.

Sheraton Road Market

Location: Sheraton Road

Located in one of Hurghada's busiest tourist areas, this market is full of souvenir shops selling papyrus paintings, Egyptian cotton products, and perfume oils. It's a great place for tourists looking for more casual shopping, and there's plenty of variety in terms of products and prices.

Senzo Mall

Location: South of Hurghada

Although it's a modern mall, Senzo Mall offers a mix of local shops and larger stores selling traditional Egyptian souvenirs, perfumes, and handicrafts. There are several shops in the mall that sell Egyptian cotton products and other clothing that are locally designed; hence, the shops are very comfortable for shoppers.

Hurghada Marina Bazaar

Location: Hurghada Marina

The bazaar at the Hurghada Marina is a quieter, more relaxed place to shop for souvenirs. The stalls here offer unique finds, such as handmade jewelry, artisanal candles, and handwoven baskets. The marina is also a scenic spot to enjoy the view while shopping.

Best Places to Buy Art and Crafts

For visitors who are interested in buying some arts and crafts that are made in Egypt, Hurghada has a lot of galleries, craft markets and artisan shops. These are very ideal for those who would like to be able to take some memorable and special pieces home..

Top Spots for Art and Crafts:

Mini Egypt Park (Gift Shop)

Location: Makadi Bay

Mini Egypt Park not only offers an impressive collection of miniature landmarks but also has a gift shop that sells local crafts inspired by Egyptian history. The shop features handmade figurines, traditional pottery, and Egyptian-themed artwork, all of which make for unique souvenirs.

Contemporary Art Gallery El Gouna

Location: El Gouna

This gallery showcases a diverse range of artwork by Egyptian and international artists, including paintings, sculptures, and photography. It's an excellent place to buy original pieces of art, as well as smaller items like hand-painted ceramics and artisan jewelry.

Website: www.artgalleryelgouna.com

Hurghada Artisan Crafts Market

Location: Downtown Hurghada

This local market is focused on showcasing the work of local artisans, with stalls selling handmade leather goods, woven rugs, metalwork, and traditional Bedouin crafts. It's a great place to find one-of-a-kind pieces while supporting local craftsmanship.

Egyptian Handicraft Village

Location: El Kawther District

Known for its high-quality handcrafted items, the Handicraft Village offers a selection of embroidered textiles, ceramics, silver jewelry, and woven baskets. Many of the items here are made by local artisans, and you can often watch the crafting process as you shop.

El Gouna Art Village

Location: El Gouna

This art village offers a unique blend of modern and traditional artwork. Visitors can buy paintings, hand-painted pottery, and glass art, all created by local artists. The village also holds regular art workshops for those interested in learning local techniques.

Supporting Local Businesses

Shopping at local businesses is not only a great way to find unique products, but it also helps to support

Hurghada's economy and sustain local craftspeople. Whether you're buying handmade souvenirs or dining at locally owned restaurants, you can make a positive impact by prioritizing local shops.

How to Support Local Businesses

Buy Handmade Souvenirs: When purchasing souvenirs, opt for items made by local artisans rather than mass-produced products. Handmade goods, such as woven baskets, pottery, and textiles, are often more unique and contribute directly to the livelihoods of local craftspeople.

Dine at Local Restaurants: Instead of eating at international chains, try local restaurants that serve authentic Egyptian cuisine. Restaurants like El Halaka and El Dar Darak are locally owned and offer delicious, traditional dishes. Supporting these businesses helps preserve Egypt's culinary heritage.

Purchase Fair Trade Products: Look for fair trade items, such as coffee, spices, and handcrafted goods, which ensure that the artisans are paid fairly for their work. Many local shops in Hurghada offer fair trade products, allowing you to make more ethical purchases.

Shop at Local Markets: Visiting local markets is a great way to interact with local sellers and artisans. It's an opportunity to learn more about Egyptian culture while directly supporting small businesses. Markets like El Dahar Souk or the Hurghada Artisan Crafts Market are ideal places to find high-quality, locally made goods.

Ask About the Origins of Products: When shopping, ask vendors where the products are made. This helps you avoid purchasing imported goods and ensures that your money goes toward supporting local communities.

Chapter 16

PACKING ESSENTIALS FOR HURGHADA

Packing wisely for Hurghada ensures that you're prepared for its sunny beaches, desert adventures, and cultural experiences. This chapter outlines essential items to bring based on the weather, activities, and practical needs during your trip to Hurghada.

What to Pack for the Weather

Hurghada's climate is warm and sunny year-round, with hot summers and mild winters. Packing appropriately for the weather is essential to staying comfortable during your trip.

Essential Items for the Weather

Light, Breathable Clothing: Hurghada's temperatures can soar, especially during the summer months (May to September). Pack lightweight, breathable fabrics like cotton or linen to stay cool. Include loose-fitting tops, shorts, and dresses that offer ventilation.

Sun Protection: The Egyptian sun can be intense, so it's crucial to bring sun protection. Pack a wide-brimmed hat, sunglasses with UV protection, and a high-SPF sunscreen (preferably reef-safe for snorkeling or diving).

Tip: Don't forget lip balm with SPF and after-sun lotion for added protection.

Swimwear: Bring multiple swimsuits if you plan on spending time at the beach or pool. A cover-up or sarong is also useful when transitioning between the beach and public areas.

Light Jacket or Sweater: While Hurghada is warm, evenings can be cooler in winter (December to February), particularly near the sea. Pack a light jacket or sweater for evenings or if you plan on spending time in air-conditioned spaces.

Comfortable Footwear: For walking around markets and sightseeing, bring comfortable sandals or walking shoes. If you're planning on visiting cultural sites, closed-toe shoes might be more appropriate.

Gear for Water and Desert Activities

Hurghada is known for its outdoor adventures, from exploring coral reefs to quad biking in the desert. Make sure you're packed for both land and sea activities.

Water Activities Essentials

Reef-Safe Sunscreen: Hurghada's coral reefs are a highlight for divers and snorkelers. Pack a reef-safe sunscreen to protect your skin without harming marine life.

Snorkeling or Diving Gear: If you're an avid snorkeler or diver, you may prefer to bring your own mask, snorkel, and fins for comfort. Most tour operators provide this equipment, but having your own can enhance your experience.

Water Shoes: If you plan on wading into rocky areas or coral-rich beaches, water shoes are helpful for protecting your feet while exploring.

Dry Bag: To protect your belongings (phone, camera, wallet) while out on boats or during water activities, a dry bag is an essential item. It keeps everything dry and safe from water damage.

Desert Activities Essentials

Desert-Ready Footwear: If you're planning on quad biking, camel riding, or hiking in the desert, bring sturdy, closed-toe shoes with a good grip to protect your feet from the hot sand and rocky terrain.

Headscarf or Bandana: To protect yourself from sand and the sun during desert excursions, bring a headscarf or bandana. Many travelers opt for the traditional keffiyeh, which can also be purchased locally.

Sunglasses with UV Protection: The sun in the desert is strong, so make sure your sunglasses offer 100% UV protection to shield your eyes from the glare.

Lightweight Backpack: For day trips and desert excursions, a small, lightweight backpack is ideal for carrying essentials like water, snacks, and sunscreen.

Packing for Cultural Activities

While Hurghada is more relaxed than other parts of Egypt, it's still important to pack culturally appropriate clothing for excursions to traditional areas or religious sites.

Essentials for Cultural Activities

Modest Clothing: If you're visiting mosques, temples, or local villages, pack clothing that covers your shoulders and knees. Women may want to bring long skirts or loose pants and scarves to cover their hair when visiting religious sites.

Comfortable Shoes for Walking: Many cultural activities, such as exploring Hurghada's markets or touring ancient sites, require a fair amount of walking. Comfortable, closed-toe shoes or sturdy sandals are recommended.

Scarf or Shawl: A lightweight scarf can be useful for covering up in religious places or when temperatures drop in the evening.

Tip: In tourist-heavy areas like the Marina or resorts, the dress code is more relaxed, but it's still respectful to dress modestly when visiting local neighborhoods.

Travel Insurance and Medical Kit

Preparing for unexpected situations while traveling is essential, and packing a small medical kit along with travel insurance details ensures you're ready for any minor emergencies.

Travel Insurance Considerations

Keep a Copy of Your Insurance: Always carry a digital or printed copy of your travel insurance policy, including the company's emergency contact information. Make sure your policy covers any adventure activities you plan to do, such as scuba diving, desert safaris, or water sports.

Health Insurance: If you have specific medical needs, bring any necessary documentation or letters from your doctor. Ensure that your travel insurance covers emergency medical treatment and evacuations, as healthcare in private hospitals can be expensive without insurance.

Medical Kit Essentials

Basic First Aid Supplies: Bring a small first aid kit that includes band-aids, antiseptic wipes, gauze, tweezers, and antibiotic ointment for minor cuts or scrapes.

Prescription Medications: If you take any prescription medications, ensure you have enough for your entire trip, plus a few extra days in case of delays. Keep medications in their original packaging, along with a copy of the prescription.

Over-the-Counter Medicines: Consider bringing common over-the-counter medications such as pain relievers, motion sickness tablets, anti-diarrheal medication, and antihistamines for allergies.

Insect Repellent: While mosquitoes aren't a major concern in Hurghada, it's still wise to pack insect repellent for evenings, especially if you're near the water or taking a desert trip.

Rehydration Salts: Dehydration can be a concern in the desert climate, so pack oral rehydration salts or electrolyte tablets to stay hydrated if you're spending a lot of time outdoors.

Chapter 17

MONEY AND CURRENCY IN HURGHADA

Understanding how to manage your money while traveling in Hurghada will help ensure that you can navigate payments, tipping, and currency exchange with ease. This chapter provides an overview of using Egyptian pounds, accessing ATMs, and tipping etiquette in Hurghada.

Using Egyptian Pounds and Payment Options

The official currency in Egypt is the Egyptian pound (EGP), denoted by the symbol £E or LE (Livre Egyptienne). The Egyptian pound is divided into 100 piastres. It's important to use local currency for most transactions, though credit cards are widely accepted in larger establishments.

Key Points About Using Egyptian Pounds

Cash Is Preferred: While credit and debit cards are accepted in hotels, larger restaurants, and shops, cash is still king in Egypt. Small vendors, markets, taxis, and local restaurants often only accept cash, so it's wise to carry small denominations of Egyptian pounds for everyday expenses.

Currency Denominations: Banknotes come in denominations of 5, 10, 20, 50, 100, and 200 pounds. Coins are available for smaller amounts (1, 5, and 10 piastres), though smaller denominations are less commonly used in daily transactions.

Foreign Currencies: In some tourist-heavy areas, such as resorts and larger hotels, prices may be quoted in euros or US dollars. However, it's best to pay in Egyptian pounds to avoid unfavorable exchange rates or confusion.

Credit Card and ATM Access

Credit cards are widely accepted in most hotels, restaurants, and larger shops in Hurghada, though smaller businesses and markets usually only accept cash. ATMs are easy to find throughout the city and can be used to withdraw local currency.

Tips for Using Credit Cards and ATMs

Accepted Credit Cards: Most major credit cards, including Visa, Mastercard, and American Express, are accepted at larger hotels, upscale restaurants, and shops. Always check with the merchant before assuming credit cards are accepted, especially in smaller establishments.

ATM Access: Hurghada has a large number of ATMs, particularly in tourist areas like the Marina, Sheraton Road, and major hotels. ATMs typically allow you to withdraw Egyptian pounds directly from your foreign bank account, though there may be additional fees.

Tip: If you're withdrawing cash from an ATM, it's recommended to withdraw larger sums at once to avoid multiple transaction fees. Keep small bills on hand for taxis, tips, and market purchases.

Currency Conversion Fees: When using a credit card or ATM, check if your bank applies foreign transaction fees or conversion charges. These fees can add up, so it's a good idea to contact your bank before your trip to understand their policies and consider using a travel credit card with no foreign transaction fees.

Tipping and Service Charges

Tipping is an integral part of Egyptian culture and is expected in many service situations. Tipping, or "baksheesh", is often given in addition to service charges, which are sometimes included in restaurant or hotel bills.

Tipping Guidelines in Hurghada

Restaurants: While many restaurants include a service charge (typically 10-12%), this fee often goes to the establishment, not the staff. It's customary to leave an additional 5-10% for the server as a tip. In smaller or local restaurants, you may round up the bill or leave a few pounds as a tip.

Hotels: When staying at a hotel, tip porters around 10-20 EGP per bag and leave 20-30 EGP per day for housekeeping. If the hotel staff provides additional services (such as arranging tours or offering special assistance), tipping is appreciated.

Taxis: It's common to round up the fare when using taxis in Hurghada, especially if the driver has provided good service. A tip of 5-10 EGP is usually sufficient for short trips.

Tour Guides and Drivers: For guided tours, tipping the guide and driver is customary. For a half-day tour, a tip of around 50-100 EGP per person for the guide and 20-50 EGP for the driver is standard. For longer or private tours, tips may be higher.

Tip: Always carry small bills for tipping purposes, as it can be difficult for service staff to provide change.

Where to Exchange Money Safely

Exchanging money in Hurghada is generally straightforward, and it's important to know where to go to get the best rates and avoid scams. There are several safe and convenient options for currency exchange.

Best Places to Exchange Money

Banks

Banks in Hurghada offer competitive exchange rates and are a reliable place to exchange foreign currency into Egyptian pounds. Banque Misr, National Bank of Egypt, and CIB (Commercial International Bank) are among the most prominent banks with branches across the city.

Tip: Banks are typically open from Sunday to Thursday, 8:30 AM to 2:00 PM.

Currency Exchange Offices

Hurghada has several licensed exchange offices where you can exchange money. These offices are usually located in tourist areas like Sheraton Road and the Marina. Exchange rates here are competitive, and transactions are quick and easy.

Examples of reputable currency exchange offices include Thomas Cook Exchange and El Gouna Exchange.

ATMs

Many ATMs in Hurghada allow you to withdraw Egyptian pounds directly from your home bank account, usually at the current exchange rate with minimal fees. HSBC, Banque Misr, and CIB are common ATM providers in the city.

Tip: Avoid withdrawing large amounts of money from ATMs late at night or in less secure areas. Stick to well-lit, populated areas like hotels or malls.

Airport Currency Exchange

Currency exchange services are available at Hurghada International Airport, but the exchange rates here may not be as favorable as in the city. It's a convenient option if you need cash upon arrival, but it's better to exchange larger amounts once you're in town.

What to Avoid

Avoid Street Money Changers: Though you may find street vendors offering to exchange money, it's best to avoid these unofficial exchanges. They may offer unfavorable rates or even counterfeit currency. Stick to official exchange offices or banks for safety.

Keep Receipts: When exchanging money at banks or exchange offices, keep your receipt. This will be useful if you plan to change any leftover Egyptian pounds back to your home currency when leaving Egypt.

Chapter 18

LANGUAGE AND COMMUNICATION

While Arabic is the official language of Egypt, you'll find that English is widely spoken in tourist areas like Hurghada. Learning a few Arabic phrases and understanding local communication norms can greatly enhance your travel experience. This chapter covers the basics of Arabic for travelers, common phrases, and tools to help with translation.

Arabic Basics for Travelers

In Egypt, Modern Standard Arabic is the official language used in formal settings such as media, schools, and government. However, Egyptian Arabic, also known as Masri, is the local dialect spoken by the majority of Egyptians in everyday conversations. It's helpful to learn a few basic phrases in Egyptian Arabic to show respect and communicate with locals.

Key Arabic Basics for Travelers

Hello: "Salam" (سلام) or "Marhaba" (مرحبا)

Good Morning: "Sabah el kheir" (صباح الخير)

Good Evening: "Masaa el kheir" (مساء الخير)

Thank You: "Shukran" (شكرا)

You're Welcome: "Afwan" (عفوا)

Please: "Min fadlak" (من فضلك) [for a man] / "Min fadlik" [for a woman]

Yes: "Na'am" (نعم)

No: "La" (لا)

Excuse Me / Sorry: "Asif" (آسف) [for a man] / "Asifa" [for a woman]

How Much?: "Bikam?" (بكم؟)

Where is...?: "Fein...?" (فين...؟)

Even though many locals in tourist areas will speak English, using these Arabic phrases can help build rapport and make your interactions more friendly and respectful.

Common Phrases You'll Need

When exploring Hurghada, especially in markets, restaurants, or when asking for directions, certain Arabic phrases will come in handy. Here are some common phrases you might find useful during your trip.

Common Travel Phrases

Do you speak English?: "Bitkallem Englizi?" (بتتكلم إنجليزي؟)

How are you?: "Ezayak?" (إزيك؟) [for a man] / "Ezayik?" [for a woman]

I'm fine, thank you: "Ana kowayyes, shukran" (أنا كويس شكرا) [for a man] / "Ana kwayessa, shukran" [for a woman]

Can you help me?: "Momken tsaedni?" (ممكن تساعدني؟)

How much is this?: "Bikam da?" (بكم ده؟)

I would like this: "Ana ayez da" (أنا عايز ده) [for a man] / "Ana ayza di" [for a woman]

What is your name?: "Esmak eh?" (اسمك ايه؟)

My name is…: "Ismi…" (اسمي...)

I don't understand: "Ana mish fahem" (أنا مش فاهم) [for a man] / "Ana mish fahma" [for a woman]

Where is the bathroom?: "Fein el hammam?" (فين الحمام؟)

Goodbye: "Ma'a as-salama" (مع السلامة)

Phrases for Shopping and Markets:

Can you give me a discount?: "Momken tedi li khisam?" (ممكن تديني خصم؟)

It's too expensive: "Da ghali awi" (ده غالي قوي)

I'm just looking: "Ana bas botforrag" (أنا بس بتفرج)

Learning these basic phrases can help you navigate daily interactions more smoothly, especially in local markets where haggling is common.

English vs. Arabic: Where It's Spoken

While Arabic is the national language of Egypt, English is widely spoken in tourist-friendly areas, especially in Hurghada, which welcomes millions of international visitors each year. Here's where you can expect to hear English versus where Arabic might be more prevalent.

Where English is Common

Hotels and Resorts: Most hotel staff, particularly in large resorts and international hotel chains, speak English fluently. Front desk staff, concierge services, and restaurant servers will often greet you in English and handle most requests in English.

Restaurants and Cafés: In tourist areas, many menus are available in both English and Arabic, and restaurant staff are used to interacting with English-speaking visitors.

Tour Operators and Guides: Many tour companies in Hurghada cater to international visitors, so guides usually speak fluent English. They will often conduct tours in English or offer multilingual services.

Shops in Tourist Areas: Most shop owners in the Marina or popular tourist streets, like Sheraton Road, will speak basic English to help with transactions. Prices may also be quoted in both Egyptian pounds and other currencies like euros or dollars.

Where Arabic is More Common

Local Markets: While some English is spoken in the more tourist-oriented parts of Hurghada's markets, smaller, local markets may have more Arabic speakers.

Using basic Arabic phrases can make these interactions smoother.

Public Transportation: If you're using local transportation such as shared taxis (known as "microbuses") or traveling to areas outside Hurghada, you may find that drivers and passengers speak mostly Arabic.

Traditional Neighborhoods: In more residential or traditional parts of Hurghada, Arabic will be the primary language used. However, locals are often accommodating and may speak basic English, especially to assist visitors.

Apps and Tools to Help with Translation

In today's digital age, you don't need to be fluent in Arabic to get by in Hurghada. Several translation apps and tools can help you communicate with locals and understand signs, menus, or conversations.

Recommended Translation Apps

Google Translate

Features: Google Translate allows you to translate text, speech, and even live images (such as menus or signs) from Arabic to English and vice versa. You can also download the Arabic language pack for offline use, which is useful if you're in areas with limited internet access.

Available on: Android and iOS.

Microsoft Translator

Features: Microsoft Translator supports voice, text, and image translations and works well for everyday conversations. It also has a conversation mode that can translate back and forth in real-time, making it easier to communicate with locals.

Available on: Android and iOS.

Arabic Dictionary & Translator by Bravolol

Features: This app is specifically designed for travelers and features a phrasebook with common travel phrases in Arabic and English. It also provides offline functionality, so you can use it even without an internet connection.

Available on: Android and iOS.

iTranslate

Features: iTranslate is another useful app for translating speech and text in real-time. It also offers offline translation features and a voice-to-voice conversation mode, which can be especially helpful in markets or local restaurants.

Available on: Android and iOS.

Other Useful Tools

Phrasebooks: Consider carrying a small Arabic-English phrasebook for quick reference. These are particularly helpful when you don't have access to internet or translation apps.

Language Learning Apps: If you want to learn more Arabic phrases before your trip, apps like Duolingo or Memrise offer easy-to-use lessons focused on basic travel vocabulary.

Chapter 19

PRACTICAL TRAVEL TIPS

Traveling to Hurghada is exciting, but knowing the practical details can make your trip smoother and more enjoyable. This chapter covers essential travel information, from electricity and internet access to health requirements and local emergency contacts, ensuring that you're well-prepared for your visit.

Electricity and Plug Types

Before traveling to Hurghada, it's essential to understand the local electricity system to ensure your devices can be charged or used without issues.

Electricity Specifications

Voltage: 220V

Frequency: 50Hz

Plug Types:

Egypt uses the **Type C** and **Type F** plug types, which have two round pins. These are the same as those used in much of Europe.

Type C: Two round pins

Type F: Two round pins with grounding clips on the side

If your devices use a different type of plug, you will need to bring a plug adapter. Additionally, if your devices do not support 220V, a voltage converter will be necessary.

Tip: Many hotels in Hurghada may offer international plug points or adapters, but it's always a good idea to bring your own to avoid any inconvenience.

Internet and SIM Cards

Having access to reliable internet is important for staying connected, navigating the city, and using translation apps. In Hurghada, you'll find several options for internet access, including free Wi-Fi at hotels and local SIM cards for more reliable data use.

Internet Access

Hotel Wi-Fi: Most hotels and resorts in Hurghada offer free Wi-Fi in public areas like lobbies and lounges. However, in-room Wi-Fi may come with additional charges or have limited speeds, so it's worth confirming Wi-Fi availability when booking.

Cafés and Restaurants: Many cafés and restaurants, especially in tourist areas such as the Marina or Sheraton Road, offer free Wi-Fi. Ask staff for the Wi-Fi password when ordering.

Local SIM Cards

Purchasing a local SIM card is an affordable way to ensure you have data access throughout your trip, especially when exploring outside of Wi-Fi zones. SIM cards can be purchased at the airport or at mobile shops in the city.

Major Providers: Egypt has three main mobile providers—Vodafone, Orange, and Etisalat. Each offers prepaid SIM cards with data packages that can be tailored to your needs (e.g., internet only, or combined with calling/texting options).

Documents Needed: You'll need your passport to purchase a SIM card, as it must be registered to your name.

Coverage: All three providers offer good coverage in Hurghada, but Vodafone is often considered to have the most reliable service in tourist areas.

Tip: Make sure your phone is unlocked to use a local SIM card. You can also top up data easily at kiosks or through apps offered by the mobile providers.

Local Emergency Contacts

Knowing local emergency numbers and having the necessary contact information is crucial during your trip. Egypt's emergency services are available for both tourists and locals, and most hotels and tour operators will have additional contact information in case of emergencies.

Key Emergency Numbers in Hurghada

Ambulance: 123

Police: 122

Fire Department: 180

Tourist Police: 126

The Tourist Police are specially designated to assist tourists with issues such as lost passports, theft, and harassment. They are generally stationed in key tourist areas and often speak English.

Embassy Contacts

If you require assistance from your embassy, it's important to have their contact details on hand. Major embassies are located in Cairo, but consular services may be available for emergencies in Hurghada.

British Embassy in Cairo

Phone: +20 2 2791 6000

Website: www.gov.uk/world/organisations/british-embassy-cairo

U.S. Embassy in Cairo

Phone: +20 2 2797 3300

Website: eg.usembassy.gov

German Embassy in Cairo

Phone: +20 2 2728 2000

Website: kairo.diplo.de

Health and Vaccination Requirements

Egypt does not require any mandatory vaccinations for entry, but it's always best to be up to date on routine vaccinations before you travel. In some cases, additional vaccinations may be recommended depending on the activities you plan to engage in and the areas you'll be visiting.

Recommended Vaccinations

Routine Vaccinations: Ensure that you're up to date on standard vaccines, including measles-mumps-rubella (MMR), diphtheria-tetanus-pertussis, varicella (chickenpox), polio, and influenza.

Hepatitis A: Recommended for most travelers, as you can get hepatitis A through contaminated food or water in Egypt.

Hepatitis B: Recommended for those who might be exposed to blood or bodily fluids (e.g., healthcare workers), or those engaging in adventure activities.

Typhoid: Recommended for travelers staying in more rural areas or who may eat street food, as typhoid can spread through contaminated food and water.

Rabies: Although rabies is not a major concern in urban Hurghada, travelers participating in outdoor activities like hiking or exploring rural areas may want to consider this vaccination.

Water Safety

Tap Water: Tap water in Egypt is not safe to drink, so always stick to bottled water. Ensure that bottles are sealed before purchasing, and use bottled water for brushing your teeth.

Food Safety: Stick to food from reputable restaurants and avoid eating raw or undercooked meats. Peel fruits and wash vegetables with bottled water if you're preparing your own meals.

Tip: If you require prescription medication, bring enough for your trip and a few extra days in case of delays. Carry medications in their original packaging along with a doctor's note.

Visa and Entry Requirements for Hurghada

Travelers to Hurghada will need to ensure they meet the visa requirements for entering Egypt. Many nationalities can obtain a tourist visa upon arrival or apply for an e-visa online before traveling.

Visa Types

Tourist Visa on Arrival: Citizens from several countries, including the U.S., U.K., EU countries, Canada, and Australia, can obtain a tourist visa on arrival at Hurghada International Airport. The visa costs $25 USD and is valid for 30 days. Payment is usually made in cash (USD, euros, or GBP), and the visa is issued at the airport before you pass through immigration.

E-Visa: To save time, many travelers opt for an e-visa, which can be applied for online before arriving in Egypt. You can apply through the official Egyptian e-Visa Portal (www.visa2egypt.gov.eg). The e-visa is also valid for 30 days and costs $25 USD for a single entry.

Passport Requirements

Validity: Your passport must be valid for at least six months beyond your planned departure date from Egypt. Ensure that your passport has enough blank pages for entry and exit stamps.

Visa Extensions

If you wish to stay in Egypt for longer than 30 days, you can apply for a visa extension at the Passports, Emigration & Nationality Administration Office in Cairo. However, it's best to plan your trip within the 30-day period to avoid the need for an extension.

Chapter 20

FINAL THOUGHTS

As your journey to Hurghada draws to an end, reflecting on the positives and planning future trips might improve your entire experience. From making the most of your stay in this lovely city to practicing sustainable travel, this chapter provides closing insights to help you fully enjoy Hurghada.

Making the Most of Your Trip

To make the most of your stay in Hurghada, find a balance between rest and activity. Whether you are relaxing on the beach, discovering the rich undersea environment, or experiencing the desert, there are several ways to make the most of your vacation.

Tips for Making the Most of Your Time

Plan Ahead, but Stay Flexible: While it's good to have an itinerary, leave room for spontaneous activities.

Keep an open mind for day trips and excursions in Hurghada.

Mix Adventure and Relaxation: Hurghada offers the best of both worlds—adventurous excursions like diving and desert safaris, and tranquil experiences like lounging by the beach or exploring local markets. A mix of activities will ensure you experience all sides of the city.

Learn About Local Culture: Join locals and practice Egyptian culture. See the markets, taste traditional Egyptian food, and do cultural things such as a Bedouin dinner in the desert. These experiences will enrich your trip and create lasting memories.

Capture the Moments: Hurghada is filled with incredible landscapes, from the turquoise waters of the Red Sea to warm, golden desert sand. Remember to put down your camera and enjoy the present.

Must-See Experiences

Every traveler will experience Hurghada differently but there are certain activities that all travelers should see.

Top Must-See Experiences in Hurghada

Snorkeling or Diving in the Red Sea

Hurghada is famous for its rich marine life and crystal-clear waters. Whether you're a beginner or an experienced diver, exploring the coral reefs and underwater ecosystems of the Red Sea is a highlight of any trip. Don't miss sites like the Giftun Islands or Dolphin House.

Desert Safari and Bedouin Experience

Take a desert safari to explore the vastness of the Egyptian desert. Ride a quad bike, camel, or dune buggy and enjoy a traditional Bedouin meal under the stars. The desert offers a completely different side of Hurghada's landscape.

Relax at Hurghada Marina

Hurghada Marina is a lively area filled with restaurants, shops, and cafes. It's a great spot to unwind after a day of activities, enjoy dinner with a view, or take a boat trip along the coast.

Visit Mahmya Island

A day trip to Mahmya Island offers a peaceful retreat with white sandy beaches and pristine waters. Relax, snorkel, and enjoy the island's natural beauty—it's the perfect escape for nature lovers.

Explore El Dahar Old Town

If you want to experience real Egyptian life, head to El Dahar Old Town, enjoy the bustling market, shop around those local crafts and try the traditional food. This is a good chance to check out Hurghada outside the tourist resorts.

Planning Your Next Visit to Hurghada

Hurghada offers so much that you might not be able to fit everything into one trip. Planning a return visit allows you to explore even more of what the region has to offer. Whether it's diving deeper into the Red Sea's marine life or visiting nearby cities, there's always something new to discover.

Ideas for Your Next Trip

Explore Nearby Cities: On your next visit, consider taking day trips to nearby cities like Luxor, where you can visit the Valley of the Kings and the Karnak Temple, or Cairo, to see the Pyramids of Giza and the Egyptian Museum.

Extend Your Stay for Cultural Immersion: If you didn't have time to explore Hurghada's cultural aspects, dedicate part of your next trip to deeper cultural immersion. You can join a traditional cooking class, visit more historical sites, or take a multi-day desert expedition.

Experience Different Seasons: Each season brings different experiences to Hurghada. If you visited in the summer, plan your next trip in the cooler months (October to April), when the weather is milder, perfect for outdoor activities and desert tours.

Try New Adventures: Hurghada is constantly evolving as a travel destination, offering new activities and excursions. Consider returning for a kitesurfing or windsurfing course, or participate in eco-friendly tours that emphasize sustainable travel.

Encouraging Responsible and Sustainable Travel

Sustainable travel practices help preserve Hurghada's natural environment and cultural heritage for future generations. As tourism continues to grow in the region, it's important to be a responsible traveler and contribute positively to the local community.

Tips for Sustainable Travel

Support Local Businesses: Buy from local markets, dine at locally-owned restaurants, and hire local guides. Supporting local businesses ensures that the community benefits directly from tourism.

Respect Wildlife and Natural Areas: When diving or snorkeling, avoid touching coral reefs or disturbing marine life. Stick to marked paths when hiking in the desert, and minimize your impact on the environment by taking all litter with you.

Choose Eco-Friendly Accommodations and Tours: Opt for hotels, resorts, and tour operators that practice sustainability, such as reducing plastic use, conserving water, or engaging in environmental initiatives like beach clean-ups.

Minimize Waste: Bring a reusable water bottle, avoid using single-use plastics, and reduce waste wherever possible. Many resorts and shops offer filtered water stations where you can refill your bottle.

Educate Yourself and Others: Learn about the local culture and environmental challenges in Hurghada, and spread awareness about responsible travel practices. By educating yourself, you become a more informed traveler and can encourage others to travel responsibly.

Chapter 21

APPENDIX

The appendix contains some of the Hurghada information that is likely to be useful to you in the course of your stay such as the emergency contacts and the addresses of some of the establishments that you are likely to visit during your trip to Hurghada. This section will be a useful reference to help you navigate the city, find important services, and explore local sites.

Emergency Contacts

Ambulance: 123

Police: 122

Fire Department: 180

Tourist Police: 126

The Tourist Police are available in major tourist areas to assist travelers with issues such as lost passports, theft, or any security concerns.

British Embassy in Cairo

Phone: +20 2 2791 6000

Website: www.gov.uk/world/organisations/british-embassy-cairo

U.S. Embassy in Cairo

Phone: +20 2 2797 3300

German Embassy in Cairo

Phone: +20 2 2728 2000

Maps and Navigational Tools

For navigating Hurghada, online maps and GPS tools are invaluable. Here are some options for getting around:

Google Maps: Google Maps offers reliable directions and route planning for Hurghada, including public transport options and walking routes.

Website: www.maps.google.com

MAPS.ME: This app offers downloadable maps for offline use, which is useful when exploring areas without internet access. It provides detailed routes for walking and driving.

Website: www.maps.me

CityMaps2Go: An offline map app that allows you to download maps and guides for Hurghada, including recommendations for top attractions, restaurants, and hotels.

Website: www.citymaps2go.com

Additional Reading and References

To deepen your understanding of Egypt's history, culture, and travel tips, here are some recommended resources:

"Egypt: A Short History" by Robert L. Tignor

A comprehensive history of Egypt from ancient times to the present.

"Lonely Planet Egypt"

A trusted travel guide offering in-depth information on travel tips, history, and culture, including sections on Hurghada and the Red Sea.

"**The Rough Guide to Egypt**"

Another excellent travel guide with practical advice, itineraries, and detailed information about Hurghada.

"**Travels in Egypt and Nubia**" by Giovanni Belzoni

An engaging account of Belzoni's early explorations of Egypt, which includes fascinating insights into Egypt's ancient treasures.

Useful Local Phrases

Here are a few key Arabic phrases to help you communicate more easily during your stay in Hurghada:

Hello: "Salam" (سلام)

Good Morning: "Sabah el kheir" (صباح الخير)

Good Evening: "Masaa el kheir" (مساء الخير)

Thank You: "Shukran" (شكرا)

Please: "Min fadlak" (من فضلك) [for a man] / "Min fadlik" [for a woman]

How much is this?: "Bikam da?" (بكم ده؟)

Where is the bathroom?: "Fein el hammam?" (فين الحمام؟)

Goodbye: "Ma'a as-salama" (مع السلامة)

Addresses and Locations of Popular Accommodation

Steigenberger ALDAU Beach Hotel

Location: Yussif Afifi Road, Hurghada

Website: www.steigenberger.com/en/hotels/all-hotels/egypt/hurghada/steigenberger-al-dau-beach-hotel

The Oberoi Sahl Hasheesh

Location: Sahl Hasheesh, Hurghada

Website: www.oberoihotels.com/hotels-in-hurghada-sahl-hasheesh

Sheraton Miramar Resort El Gouna

Location: El Gouna, Hurghada

Website: www.marriott.com/hotels/travel/hrgsi-sheraton-miramar-resort-el-gouna

Jaz Aquamarine Resort

Location: South Sahl Hashish Road, Hurghada

Website: www.jazhotels.com/egypt/hurghada-hotels/jaz-aquamarine

Hilton Hurghada Plaza

Location: Gabal El Hareem, Hurghada

Website: www.hilton.com/en/hotels/hrghhhf-hilton-hurghada-plaza

Addresses and Locations of Popular Restaurants and Cafés

El Halaka Restaurant

Location: El Dahar Square, Hurghada

Cuisine: Egyptian, Seafood

The Lodge Restaurant & Bar

Location: Hurghada Marina

Cuisine: International

Website: www.lodgehurghada.com

Granada Restaurant & Pub

Location: Sheraton Road, Hurghada

Cuisine: Mediterranean

Website: www.granadarestaurant.com

Starfish Seafood Restaurant

Location: Sheraton Road, Hurghada

Cuisine: Seafood

Retro Pub & Grill

Location: El Mamsha Street, Hurghada

Cuisine: International, Pub

Addresses and Locations of Popular Bars and Clubs

Papas Beach Club

Location: Sheraton Road, Hurghada

Website: www.papasbeachclub.com

Little Buddha Hurghada

Location: Village Road, Hurghada

Website: www.littlebuddha-hurghada.com

Ministry of Sound Beach Club

Location: Sahl Hasheesh, Hurghada

Website: www.ministryofsound.com/egypt

Hed Kandi Beach Bar

Location: Hurghada Marina

Peanuts Bar

Location: Hilton Hurghada Plaza, Gabal El Hareem

Website: www.hilton.com/en/hotels/hrghhhf-hilton-hurghada-plaza

Addresses and Locations of Top Attractions

Giftun Islands

Location: Off the coast of Hurghada

Coordinates: 27.2154° N, 33.9948° E

Hurghada Marina

Location: Hurghada Marina Boulevard, Hurghada

Website: www.hurghadamarina.com

El Gouna

Location: 25 km north of Hurghada

Coordinates: 27.4028° N, 33.6780° E

St. Shenouda Coptic Orthodox Church

Location: El Dahar, Hurghada

Mini Egypt Park

Location: Makadi Bay, Hurghada

Website: www.miniegyptpark.com

Addresses and Locations of Clinics, Hospitals, and Pharmacies

El Gouna Hospital

Location: El Gouna, Hurghada

Website: www.elgounahospital.com

Nile Hospital Hurghada

Location: Sheraton Road, Hurghada

Website: www.nilehospitalhurghada.com

German Medical Clinic

Location: El Kawther District, Hurghada

Website: www.gmc-hurghada.com

Hurghada Hospital

Location: El Dahar, Hurghada

Red Sea Hospital

Location: Airport Road, Hurghada

Website: www.redseahospital.com

Addresses and Locations of Historical Sites

Luxor (Valley of the Kings, Karnak Temple)

Location: Luxor, approximately 290 km from Hurghada

Coordinates: 25.6872° N, 32.6396° E

Cairo (Pyramids of Giza, Egyptian Museum)

Location: Cairo, approximately 450 km from Hurghada

Coordinates: 30.0331° N, 31.2334° E

El Quseir

Location: El Quseir, approximately 140 km from Hurghada

Coordinates: 26.1055° N, 34.2779° E

Ras Mohammed National Park

Location: South Sinai, Egypt

Coordinates: 27.7306° N, 34.2564° E

St. Catherine's Monastery

Location: Sinai Peninsula

Coordinates: 28.5562° N, 33.9756° E

MAPS

Map of Hurghada

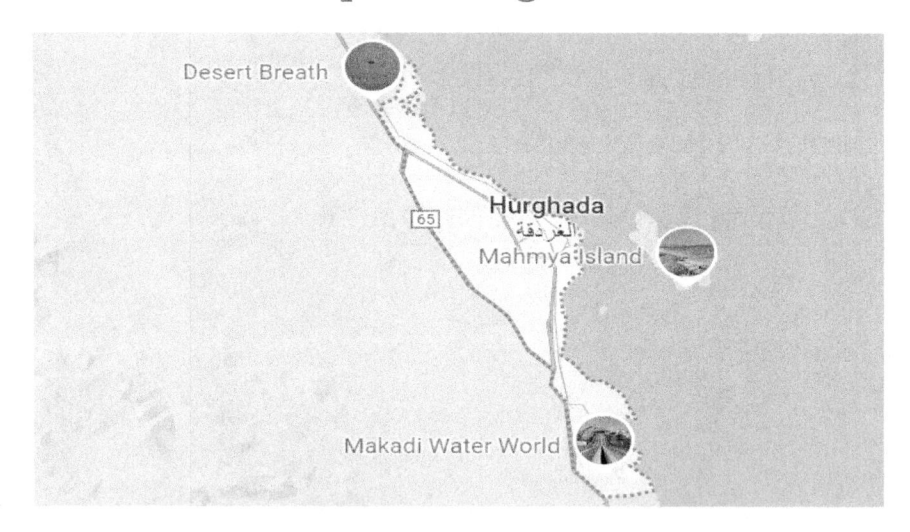

https://maps.app.goo.gl/rRHPUWE7RXiVpQjJ7

USE YOUR PHONE TO SCAN THE QR CODE IMAGE TO GET THE LOCATIONS IN REAL TIME

Things to do in Hurghada

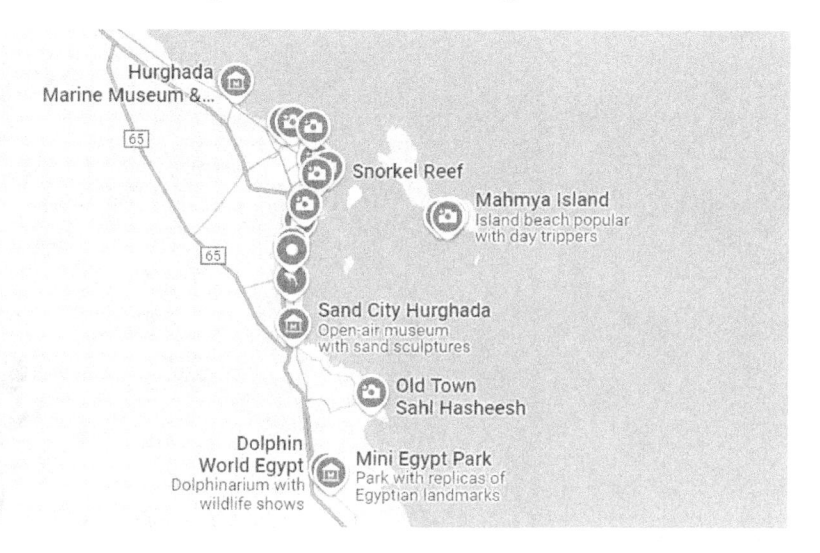

https://maps.app.goo.gl/RUwUHwaQC2BnSEx69

USE YOUR PHONE TO SCAN THE QR CODE IMAGE TO GET THE LOCATIONS IN REAL TIME

Hotels in Hurghada

https://maps.app.goo.gl/XFy5MF5B7WLEpPGM9

USE YOUR PHONE TO SCAN THE QR CODE IMAGE TO GET THE LOCATIONS IN REAL TIME

Vacation Rentals in Hurghada

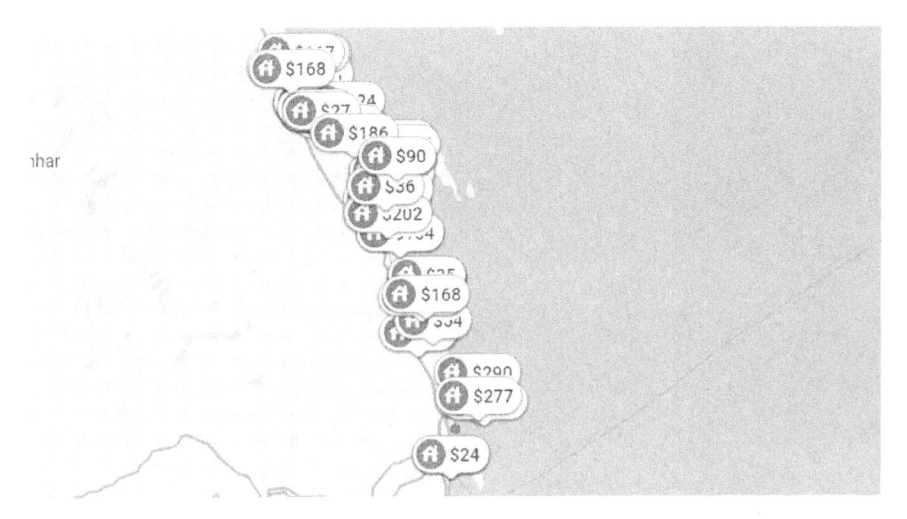

https://maps.app.goo.gl/HwvMh2PGK1bPWkpJ9

USE YOUR PHONE TO SCAN THE QR CODE IMAGE TO GET THE LOCATIONS IN REAL TIME

Restaurants in Hurghada

https://maps.app.goo.gl/E6B7DVAtHKNVoDvb9

USE YOUR PHONE TO SCAN THE QR CODE IMAGE TO GET THE LOCATIONS IN REAL TIME

Museums in Hurghada

https://maps.app.goo.gl/yxWf7HJTFzbo7yWz8

USE YOUR PHONE TO SCAN THE QR CODE IMAGE TO GET THE LOCATIONS IN REAL TIME

Pharmacies in Hurghada

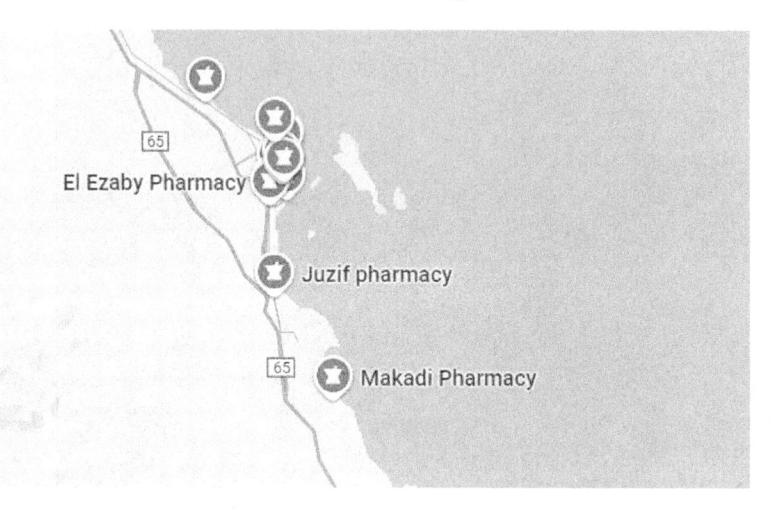

https://maps.app.goo.gl/FuybBavRMPhgeVaK7

USE YOUR PHONE TO SCAN THE QR CODE IMAGE TO GET THE LOCATIONS IN REAL TIME

ATMs in Hurghada

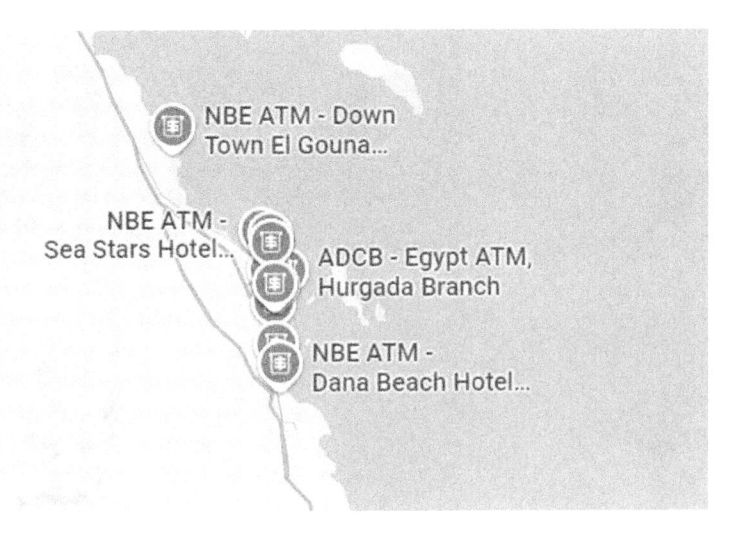

https://maps.app.goo.gl/ejzYa3jxxa1fWLjF7

USE YOUR PHONE TO SCAN THE QR CODE IMAGE TO GET THE LOCATIONS IN REAL TIME

Hiking Trails in Hurghada

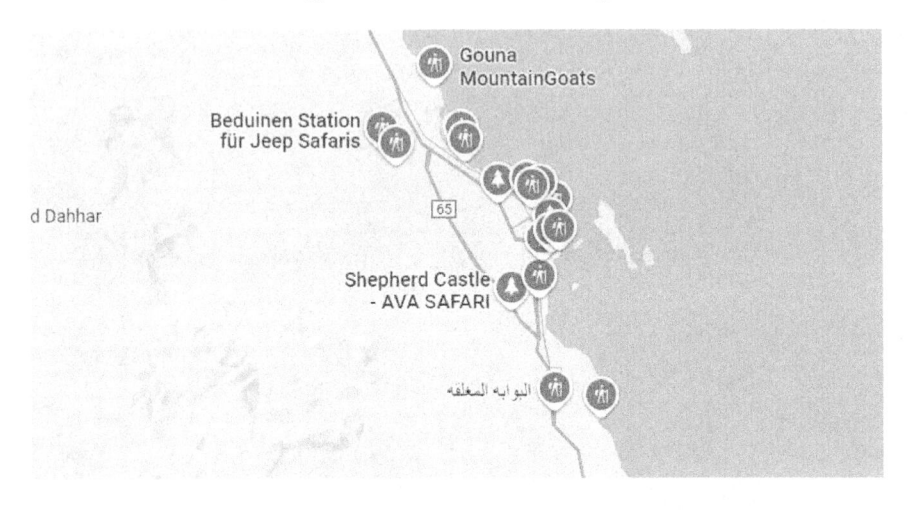

https://maps.app.goo.gl/QgzygNkEqWtmkNNi8

USE YOUR PHONE TO SCAN THE QR CODE IMAGE TO GET THE LOCATIONS IN REAL TIME

IMAGE ATTRIBUTION

https://pixabay.com/photos/egypt-hurghada-red-sea-port-mosque-796425/ (Cover page)

https://pixabay.com/photos/hotel-egypt-hurghada-red-sea-796408/ (Cover page)

APPRECIATION

Thank you so much for purchasing **Kiera Clayton's Travel Guide**! I truly appreciate your support and hope this guide helps you create amazing memories on your journey. Your feedback means the world to me, so if you found this book helpful, I would love it if you could take a moment to leave a review. Your thoughts not only help me improve, but also assist other travelers in planning their perfect trip. Thank you again, and happy travels!

Printed in Dunstable, United Kingdom